HECK&
THE DEACON

HECK & THE DEACON

Gladys King-Taylor

REVIEW AND HERALD PUBLISHING ASSOCIATION

Washington, DC 20039-0555
Hagerstown, MD 21740

Copyright © 1986 by
Review and Herald Publishing Association

This book was
Edited by Gerald Wheeler
Designed by Richard Steadham
Cover art by Nathan Greene
Type set: 11/12 Goudy

PRINTED IN U.S.A.

Library of Congress Cataloging in Publication Data

King-Taylor, Gladys, 1894-
   Heck and the Deacon.

   1.McEachern, John Hector. 2. Seventh-day Adventists
—Biography. I. Title.
BX6193.M34K56   1986   286.7'32'0924 [B]   85-18430
ISBN 0-8280-0251-7

Contents

Some will remember John McEachern for the major part he played in establishing and organizing the colporteur program in the Seventh-day Adventist Church. It was the task to which he devoted most of his life. But many of us don't read too much history or find much of interest in statistics, and so, perhaps, would never hear his name mentioned or care much about the things he did. But in Heck's story—which became John's—we find much that belongs to all of us, something to give us courage in hard times, hope in the impossible—something he would have liked to share. For that reason I have recorded it here, though sketchily and with major gaps. After all, there aren't any left who remember that morning . . .

1

"Hey, Heck." A dark-haired boy in Sunday clothes leaned over the fence.

John Hector glanced up from where he slouched against the apple tree near the corner of the yard. He didn't say anything—just looked a question.

"Chokecherries are ripe," the dark-haired boy continued in low tones. "Want to come?"

Briefly John Hector glanced toward the cabin that was his home. He didn't need to look inside. His father, Deacon Donald McEachern, would be sitting straight-backed against the log wall of the cabin reading his Gaelic Bible and waiting for the church bells to ring. (His family was too poor to have any chairs.) But it was early yet. John Hector considered the situation silently.

He was hungry. Seemed like he was always hungry. He couldn't remember ever in his whole fourteen years feeling comfortably full, and now the thought of the little black chokecherries, sweet and tangy, started things churning inside of him.

Once more he stared toward the cabin, then brushed bark dust from his Sunday pants and went out the gate. The bluffs to the rear of their homes were one of his favorite haunts, and as the boys crossed the pasture, Heck looked around with a sudden lifting of spirits. The sun had burned off the chill of the morning, and the birds were calling to one another from the woods, across the fields, and down by the stream. His long gangling legs sure of the way, he quickened his stride. The chokecherry trees would be all in one cluster up there on the hill.

"We'll have to listen for the bells, though," he warned his friend. "Father would thrash me good if I was late for Sunday school."

Bob nodded knowingly. "Reckon he would."

The chokecherries were no bigger than large cherry pits, but they grew thick among the green leaves, hanging from their long stems like little dark stars shooting out into the open. The two boys settled down to picking in silence, crunching the chokecherries until their teeth were black with the puckery juice.

His ears still tuned to the stillness of the morning, listening for those church bells, Heck thought about his father. Deacon McEachern might not be a big man physically, but what he lacked in height and build, he made up for by the stern rigidity of his life. A Calvinist to the core, he not only believed that sinners were predestined to burn forever, he also believed in keeping sin out of his household. Seemed like, Heck thought resentfully, most things were sinful. A fellow was never quite safe from the threat of the deacon's hand, and swift came the blows. Even his mother was sometimes on the receiving end of his father's wrath, and when that happened, Heck could hardly handle the anger that boiled up in him.

"Better go," Bob said suddenly.

"Bells haven't rung yet," Heck objected, his mouth full.

"No, but they're going to any minute." Bob began to clean his hands on the grass.

Heck reached for one last cherry. They were really good, and he didn't often get a treat like this. His school lunch usually consisted of no more than a dry scone made from middlings (coarse meal) his mother often received as pay for doing other people's laundry. And once, for a whole month, they had eaten nothing but potatoes and buttermilk. The boy made a face at the memory. Then, popping the last cherry into his mouth, he

8

stepped away from the shrubs and checked his Sunday pants carefully. They were clean. Glancing over at Bob, he grinned. "Your teeth are black."

"So are yours," Bob retorted. "Come on. Let's go."

They scrambled down the bluffs and ran across the pasture. About halfway to the church the clear, musical sound of a bell floated out on the air. Putting on an extra spurt, they were actually inside the building when the call to Sunday school stopped.

Not daring to look at each other, they separated, Bob going to his family, Heck looking for his father. The deacon was sitting near the front already, and as the boy approached, the man looked sternly at him. His son met his eyes squarely, then sat down on the straight-backed bench and tried to settle himself comfortably for a four-hour ordeal. Sunday school wasn't too bad, he thought. At least it had some variety. But when the preacher got up and droned on and on, it became next to impossible to keep his eyes to the front and his body still. He let his mind drift.

The morning had been beautiful out on the bluffs. Heck liked it better there than almost any place else on the island. Grand Manitoulin Island was pretty big, of course, and he hadn't ever been too far from his father's homestead cabin. Still—a smile parted his lips—those bluff chokecherries were mighty good.

Suddenly he felt his father's eyes on him. The Sunday school superintendent was getting up to announce the song, but Deacon McEachern was staring at Heck as though the boy had turned into the devil himself. For a second the boy couldn't imagine what was wrong. He looked behind him.

"It's you, boy," the deacon hissed between clenched teeth. "Your teeth are black. It's an imp of Satan you are, climbing the bluffs and eating chokecherries on the Lord's day." Anger furrowed the man's face. "I'll teach you to yield so easily to the tempter and set your very soul in peril! After church, mind you!"

Heck stood for the opening hymn, bewildered, his brain reeling. Intuition, aided by unpleasant memories, told him that his father meant to teach him with a strap in hand. Just thinking of it made his heart speed up and started the sweat oiling his hands. The instant the hymn was over and everyone knelt for prayer, he slipped noiselessly from his place, tiptoed down the aisle, and darted out the door. Once out of the church, he ran like a frightened rabbit, hoping his mother would still be home.

His feet barely touched the road, but his mind was a cauldron of anger, frustration, and fear. Unfair, his feet pounded. I was hungry. Hungry. So what's wrong with eating on the Lord's day? Unfair! Does God want me to starve? He was raging now. Wrong to hate your own father, his conscience admonished. I won't be beaten this time, his fear flamed out. I won't. I'll leave home first.

He burst through the cabin door, almost knocking his mother down. She stood there, holding to the door frame, her bonnet slightly off-center now, the question on her face. Hardly glancing at her, he headed up to his bed in the loft. There he began getting his things together.

"What is it, Heck?" she asked quietly.

"I'm leaving, Ma." Throwing his everyday shirt on the bed, he began looking for his socks. His hands trembled and he fumbled with everything he touched. "I'm not going to take it any longer. He can't thrash me again. He—" Heck stifled the flood of words and glanced down the ladder. His mother was still standing there.

"What happened, son?" Her voice was barely audible.

"All I did was go with Bob to the bluff for chokecherries. We were hungry, Ma. Does that make us 'imps of Satan'?" Unconsciously, his intonation took on his father's condemning tones. "He said he would teach me—" Heck turned back and began rolling up his clothes. "But he won't. Not this time. I'm leaving."

She did not answer, and when he tucked his bundle under

his arm and headed down for the door, she had a small paper package for him.

"Scones," she explained, handing it to him. "Where will you go?"

His anger began to ebb under her gentleness, and though he didn't see the hurt in her, he felt a little uneasy, as though there were something else here he didn't quite understand. But he shrugged it off. "I'll find work somewhere, Ma. I'll be OK."

She nodded, but said nothing. "I'll be all right," he repeated helplessly, then brushed past her and went out into the sunshine. The boy didn't look back, for unexplainably, he was now angry at her, too—angry for feeling uneasy and unsure. He wished she had scolded him, tried to stop him. Then he could have vented his anger on her.

"She chose to marry him," he muttered to himself. "She can stay, but I *won't*. I didn't choose him for my father. I didn't choose to be *born*, either. I've got to put up with that, but I won't put up with him." His stride quickened as he realized that the deacon might appear at any time. Half-fearfully he glanced over his shoulder, but saw no one. The dirt road stretched out empty behind him, and the great stretch of woods all along it stirred up a memory from the recesses of his mind.

He was very little, trudging the three-mile trek to school on a winter morning. His feet left small imprints in the freshly fallen snow. Looking up once, his heart had popped right up into his throat. There in the path before him had stood some kind of animal, big and furry, staring straight at him. Heck had frozen on the spot, too terrified to move. They had faced each other for eternity, then the animal had turned and walked slowly into the woods. The boy had streaked for home, his heart still thumping in his throat.

Ma hadn't been much of a refuge that day, he reflected now as he hurried to put more distance between him and home. She had wanted him in school, not running from imaginary animals. Breaking off a switch, she had marched off to school with him in tow. In spite of the misery inside Heck grinned a little to himself. Hadn't she been startled when they had come to the place where he had seen his beast, and she saw the tracks in the snow! Not many days after, he remembered, he had met his creature again, farther off, but not willing to leave so easily this time. The big thing had kept creeping closer until when about eight feet away, it had tensed, ready to spring. Heck had done then what his mother had taught him to do in trouble—he had prayed for help. Again, unexplainably, the animal had turned and walked into the woods. Not caring to be switched again, the boy had run all the way to school.

Now he shook off the memory. No place to flee to now. He was on his own, and he had to find his own way. In his anger it had seemed easy. Now he wasn't so sure. His insides were getting hollow, and those scones wouldn't go very far.

The road was still empty behind him, but off in the woods he saw a creek spilling down a rise and disappearing under tangled brush. Leaving the road, he sat down. His feet hurt where his Sunday shoes rubbed them. Pulling them off, he tossed them to one side. The socks followed, and he slid his feet gratefully into the water.

Feet in the water, he munched the dry scones and wished for something more. Although he was used to being only half full, it didn't mean that he didn't dream of other things—turkey roasting on the fire, mounds of mashed potatoes with butter melting into puddles, fresh green peas from the garden cooked with tiny, clear onions. Thinking about food made him remember Charles. Abruptly he pulled his feet out of the water and brushed away crumbs. He didn't want to think about the boy.

Heck trudged on down the road, noticing that the maple leaves were just beginning to color some of the trees. Barefoot now, he had rolled his Sunday shoes into his bundle. His feet felt a lot better, free like this, sinking into the dust of the road. Funny how Charles had been just fine until he'd started coughing, getting thinner, tiring easily. They'd had turkey at the boy's house, and potatoes and peas—so many good things.

"Let's take our lunch out under the trees," Charles would say at noon at school. "Maybe we'll see an eagle, or a fox, or a snake." Had his mother ever wondered why her son needed so many sandwiches? Heck kicked at a stick in the road. Charles was dead. No use thinking about it. He trudged on.

By late afternoon he was really hungry. No one had followed him or tried to force him back home, and his anger had drained away. Tired, he was beginning to worry a little.

"Where are you headed, son?"

The voice came from a fenced-in field, and Heck looked over at its owner. The farmer seemed friendly enough, not pushy.

"Looking for work," the boy answered slowly.

The farmer took off his hat and scratched his head. Aware of the eyes that looked him over from cowlick to bare, dusty feet, Heck straightened up a little, but didn't say anything.

"And supposing I gave you work," the man said thoughtfully. "Supposing you fed my cattle and I found you a bed and three square meals." He paused. "You want schooling, boy?"

Heck was surprised. School? He hadn't even given a thought to that, but yes. "Yes, sir. I'd like that if . . ." Not sure yet what the offer would be, he stopped.

"You feed my cattle mornings and evenings, and I'll give you room and board, and you can go to school all you want. What do you say to that?"

A load off his mind, Heck grinned. "I say Yes. Yes, sir."

2

The maple leaves turned bright red, then faded to brown and fell from the trees. The air took on a sharpness, and one morning when Heck went out in the darkness to feed the cows and water them, snow dusted the ground. Turning up the collar of his jacket, he took the plunge into the cold. The sleeves of that jacket were a little shorter on his arms, and his shoes really pinched him now, but he didn't notice it too much. He was getting his three full meals a day and was making real progress in school. Reading fascinated him. Books were doorways, and when he opened the covers of a new one, he stepped out of this world into a completely different place. Arithmetic, geography, history, science—he waded through all of it with equal zest. He wished so much he could own a few volumes himself, but he didn't even have the money for new clothes yet.

Mr. Moore, the farmer, was a fair man, and had stuck by his bargain. Heck whistled a little and swung his empty bucket. "Move over, Betsy." He slapped the black cow on the rump, and she swished her tail almost in his face.

"Ornery thing, aren't you?" He went to the grain sack and began shaking some of it into the bucket. The cows were lowing already, anxiously watching him. "Yep," the boy said out loud. "Food for you, food for me later. Not a bad bargain." It was a relief, he thought, not to have the threat of the strap hanging over him all the time, and he certainly did not miss his father's long sermonizings on the fires of hell.

"Not that I couldn't use some fire out here today," he told

himself as he slapped his hands against his pant legs to warm himself a little. "Get in there, you stubborn old carcass you." He slapped the black cow again, and she moved over to let another one by. With all the cows in the enclosure, Heck shut the gate behind him. Forking out hay, he still had fire on his mind. The deacon's pictures of hell were far too vivid for mental comfort. Often Heck thought about Charles and wondered briefly whether his friend had been predestined to damnation. Heck tried to shake off the thought. How could a guy pray to God for help when he was eternally afraid of Him?

The cows in the dark mornings. Breakfast, with hot oatmeal steaming in bowls, and fresh cold milk to pour over it. Plenty of bread and butter to fill a guy's empty insides. School. Chores. Study. Falling asleep as soon as the candle was blown out. Heck lost track of the days.

The ice melted. The snow blew away. The first clear song of a robin caught him totally by surprise. So did the man in the chair by the kitchen one day when Heck came in from school.

"Time you came home, boy," Deacon McEachern said shortly.

Heck stood motionless—the taste of acid in his throat, thoughts floating across his brain but gone before he could find the words for them—and he could only look helplessly toward the farmer who had taken him in.

"He's your father, lad," Mr. Moore told him "You'd best go with him."

"No best about it," the deacon retorted sharply. "He's got no choice."

Wordlessly, the boy went for his clothes and once more rolled them into a bundle. Silently he came back to the room and faced his father.

Behind him the farmer spoke, still trying to ease the situation. "You've been a help, lad. We'll miss you."

Heck nodded, knowing he was being rude, knowing he should thank the man, but still the words wouldn't come. Then he followed his father out the door and didn't look back.

"Now that you've made yourself a worker, you can earn some cash," his father told him on the way home. "I've hired you out to Mr. Williams for seven dollars a month."

Money. Cash. Heck turned the thought over in his mind. That wouldn't be so bad. He needed clothes desperately. He'd worn these same ones since the day he'd left home. They were now like the rags his mother poked into crevices between the logs of the cabin to keep out the snow and the biting wind that raged in from the lakes.

Suddenly his father turned on him. "Have you no manners?" he shouted. "No respect? Not a word out of you, nor a hello or goodbye. Mind that I don't have to teach you."

Heck shrugged a little, but inside his thoughts suddenly found words. Manners? The words echoed in his head. Who are you to talk about manners? You and your sticks and straps and hellfire!

"Well?" His father had stopped in the road.

"No, sir," Heck mumbled.

And so they came home, father and son.

In some ways it was good to be home. His mother had missed him. He could see that. And suddenly he knew that he had missed her, too, though he didn't know how to tell her. Silently he watched her stirring the kettle over the fire, her brown face lined with care, her lips often pressed tightly together. Now he noticed the carefully mended shirt she had laid out for him, the cleaned shoes.

Somehow he endured the bossings he got from his father, sat silently through the long Scripture readings in the evenings, and listened to the equally long and dark commentaries his father made on them—he had done all that before. But now he tried awkwardly to do little things for his mother. He got up earlier and fixed kindling for the fire, brought in the water, was careful with his things. Although he brushed off the thanks she often tried to give him, it was good to feel appreciated.

The farm work was hard—hoeing, feeding chickens, chopping wood, plowing fields, milking cows, slopping pigs. It also seemed unending, but Heck didn't complain. He was looking forward to the day when he'd have that seven dollars in his hand.

Overalls, he thought. I've got to have a new pair. And I'll be able to get a new shirt, too. Not shoes, though. Ruefully he looked down at his bare feet. Maybe next month.

"C'mon, kid," Andrew McDonald ·laughed between mustache and beard. "Get the lead out of your heels, or I'll get it out for you." Tickled with his own wit, he laughed again.

Heck thought the joke was stale. He did speed up his hoeing, though. McDonald was big enough to take the lead out of anyone he had a mind to!

"Excuse, me," a voice said behind them.

Pausing in his hoeing, Heck glanced over his shoulder. There stood a man—wearing a suit and tie, briefcase in hand.

McDonald idled his hoe and surveyed the stranger from head to toe. "Don't mind if we do," he replied slowly, but one corner of his mouth lifted slightly. "You're decked out mighty fancy for us farm folk. What's on your mind?"

The stranger didn't seem to take offense easily. "I won't keep you long," he said quietly, "but Mr. Williams said it was OK if I spoke to you fellows a few moments."

"He's the boss," McDonald commented. "What d'you have to say that's more important than the corn? An insurance fellow?"

The visitor half smiled. "Not really, but I guess that what I have is kind of like insurance." He put down his briefcase and began to open it. Dropping his hoe, Heck walked over.

"Books!" McDonald exclaimed. "Well . . ."

Heck listened to the swearing with interest. The farm hand's vocabulary certainly was different from his father's—though, come to think of it, not all of it. Actually, it seemed as though it didn't make much difference whether you got damned in church or out on the cornfield. He shrugged.

McDonald thumbed through the book, while the stranger began his talk about the importance of the days they lived in.

Heck was more interested in the stranger than in what he had to say. The man was slight beside McDonald, but an air of sincerity and friendliness about him impressed the boy.

"Religious stuff. Pah!" His voice dripping with scorn, McDonald dropped the book back into the briefcase. "Why, you're one of them lazy-lover fellows that go around meddling in other folks' lives and trying to tell them how to go about their business." He shoved his fist right under the stranger's nose. "For a cent I'd teach you a lesson you wouldn't forget real soon." Anger crept in a red flush up his neck and across his face, his huge figure dwarfing the book salesman. Then he laughed mirthlessly. "But you're too runty to fight. Wouldn't want to hurt you none. Just pack your stuff out of here and quit interfering with a man's work!" Turning his back, the farmhand picked up his hoe.

The salesman said nothing, only looked questioningly over at Heck.

"Some time later, sir," the boy stammered. "I have no money."

The man nodded and closed the case. "What's your name, son?"

Heck swallowed. The man's voice was so kind and unruffled that he blurted out what he'd always planned to be called when he was on his own. "John. John McEachern." No Hector.

The man smiled at him. "See you sometime then, John." And left.

Heck went back to his hoe in a state of wonder. Never before had he seen a man take scorn and cursing without fighting or losing his dignity.

"John," McDonald mimicked. "Where did you dream that one up?"

"It's my other name," the boy mumbled, his ears burning.

"Yes, sir," went on McDonald, still mimicking, "but I have no money." Then roughly. "You could have told him where to take that fool religion of his."

"No call to fight him about it," Heck replied, amazed at his own daring. "I don't hold with religion any more than you, Andrew. My father preached it clean out of me, but this man was different."

"He's a good-for-nothing bum, too lazy to do honest labor, too proud of himself to work like the rest of us." After adding a few unrepeatable phrases, the farmhand lapsed into silence. Heck said nothing. His hoe chopped up and down automatically and the sweat trickled down his back, but he was lost in thought.

Payday finally came. Heck planned all morning just how and when he was going to spend those precious seven dollars. The shirt would be blue with a checkered pattern. The overalls would be routine, but at least they would be clean and whole, and they would fit. The ones he had on now were already showing ankle. He put away his tools, joined the little group in the barn, and stood in the clump of men waiting to hear his name and collect his first wages.

Finally all the men but him had received their money.

"Yes?" Mr. Williams lowered his eyebrows until they almost met above the bridge of his nose.

"My pay," Heck explained in surprise. "I came for my pay. My father said it would be seven dollars each month."

The man laughed. "He was right, son. But your father came and collected your money some time ago." Turning on his heel, he disappeared into the barn.

Heck stood rooted to the ground. The unfairness of it totally overwhelmed him. No shirt. No overalls. A month of extremely hard work, all for nothing.

"I won't stay," he decided bitterly. "I won't stand for it!"

The thought ran through his mind all evening. He said nothing to his father or mother, but the "I won'ts" hammered away at his brain. Silently he went to his bed up in the loft, but he didn't undress. Instead, he waited until he heard his father bank the fire in the stove and go into his room. Then, working silently but quickly, he packed his belongings into a little old "turkey" (a bag often used by lumbermen). Creeping down the ladder into the main room, he fixed the kindling wood his mother would need to start the fire for breakfast. Touching his mother's Bible that always lay open on a little table, he slipped out into the night.

Not far away the hollow call of a loon echoed in the rushes. He trudged through the dark down the same road he had followed before, but this time he made a decision. There would be no coming back. He was stepping out on his own, and as a sign of it, he would go by the name he had given the book agent. John McEachern. No one knew he was leaving, and probably no one except his mother would care. But he was going just the same.

The thought of his mother, left alone in the unfinished cabin to cope with the rigid demands of his deacon father, tugged at his heart, but after a moment he set it aside resolutely. She must live her life—he wanted to live his. He was a man now. A man by the name of John.

3

He walked all night. His legs began to ache after a while and, as always, hunger gnawed at his insides. But he ignored both dull pains and concentrated only on a destination. Where could he go that was beyond his father's reach? Who did he know?

As daylight began to outline the horizon, he finally settled on an idea. He would go to Tehkummah, where his sister Flora lived. Although he didn't know her very well—as all seven of his sisters had long been gone from home—maybe she would let him live with her. His pace quickened.

Flora did take him in. Actually, she was quite pleased.

"Sure, I'll call you John, Heck." She stopped and laughed. "John. And you must stay with us. You can have a bed and share our meals. There's a school close by." Bustling about the kitchen, she prepared a plate for her brother from the dinner leftovers.

Almost too tired to feel relief, he watched her. His hunger had long ago dulled into a dizzy hollowness inside him. "I'll get a job, too, Flora," he told her as he started to fork potatoes into his mouth.

"It would be a good idea," she agreed. "You need some new clothes, and a pair of shoes. Sandy's wages won't cover that." She was a bit apologetic.

John chewed and swallowed. All he wanted, suddenly, was to lie down somewhere and close his eyes. "I'll find something," he assured her. "Don't worry."

21

Flora sat down at the table. "Funny," she said thoughtfully. "You're the second person to stop by today. There was a man selling books."

Her brother looked up in surprise. "Religious books?"

"Yes. How did you know?"

"I didn't. But I met one the other day when we were working in the cornfield." John paused, remembering the man. "He was different. But really nice."

"This one was, too. I liked the book, but I was even more impressed by the man. He was a real Christian."

"It would be nice to talk to a real Christian," John said.

"I know, John. Seems like church is mostly trying to stoke up the fires of hell, but this man . . . I hope he comes back." Getting up, she began to clear the table.

He stared at her. It was strange to hear your own thoughts in the mouth of another person. And it was a kind of sharing foreign to him. "If he does come back," he said slowly, "maybe you'd better order one of his books. Wonder what they say . . ." Suddenly he yawned hugely.

Flora laughed. "Go lie down, Heck. I mean John. You're so tired I bet you couldn't remember your name, either."

Shyly he smiled at her. It was nice to be treated like a person. Maybe that didn't make sense, but it was what he was feeling, and he was too sleepy to work it out. A few minutes later he went to bed.

At Lonely Bay, a few miles away, a lumber dealer needed a man to peel the bark from cedar logs. "They're to be used for fenceposts," he explained. "Peeled, they aren't so bulky, and besides," he winked, "it costs less to ship them."

"I can do it," John assured him. "Once I get the hang of it."

"You've got yourself a job then." The lumberman held out his hand.

John took the hand, shook it, and signed himself on then and there. Entering the house the next evening, he was proud of his status. "I got a job, Flora," he announced. "Hi, Sandy," he greeted his brother-in-law.

"Sure enough?" Sandy asked the questions, but Flora looked around from the meal she was cooking.

"Yep. Peeling logs."

"They pay piece work?" Sandy continued.

"Yes." After washing his hands, John slicked a comb through his dark hair and pulled a chair up to the rough table. "By the post. But I think I can do well at it. I'll just have to put in a lot of time."

It was a new life to go with his new name, and John was happy. Mornings he went to school, then home for a good lunch. For once in his life he was getting enough to eat, and he began to lose his gaunt look and fill out a little. Afternoons he worked hard. He was strong, and the lifting and peeling became automatic movements. The stack of posts began to grow.

At home in the evenings, he ate again, then studied, for his mind was hungry too, and he wanted it filled. He couldn't believe how the days flew by, and suddenly it was payday.

The boss looked at his figures, added up a few columns, then handed him two bills—five dollars and ten dollars. John tried to keep his hand steady.

"Thank you, sir," he said.

"All yours, John. You've done a good job."

The miles home flew by under his feet. For the first time in his life he had money, real cash in his hand. He burst into the house. "Flora," he said, panting for breath. "Take care of this for me until I can get to town. I'm going to buy myself a suit of clothes and be like other boys."

"I'll do my best, John." Flashing him a smile, she put the money away in her dresser drawer, where they both thought it would be safe.

They were wrong. Sunday both Flora and John left the house. Her husband was home alone, wondering what to do with himself, when a voiced hailed him.

"Sandy, I'm going to town. Want to come along?" It was Samson, his brother. Sandy didn't even bother to invite Samson in. Shaking his head, he just stood there by the open door. "Sorry, man. Can't do it. I'd really like to, but I haven't got any money left this week."

"Look around," his brother suggested. "We haven't had a drink in a long while, and Flora's sure to have something stashed away. Look in a tumbler, in a dish—maybe in a silver-ware drawer."

Sandy searched. None of his brother's suggestions were of any help, but he finally went over to the dresser, pawed around, and came in contact with stiff paper. He pulled it out. A five and a ten.

"Hey! You were right. Here's some money!" He waved it gleefully, and Samson laughed.

"Well, let's go. What are we waiting for?"

The two men rode off to a saloon in Providence Bay, drank and drank, probably did some treating, and at the end of the day, Sandy came stumbling home. John met his brother-in-law at the gate and almost carried him in. The man was just too drunk to walk.

In the morning he was sober, but by then, Flora and her brother had discovered that the money was missing. John was sitting in the kitchen, slouched down in his chair, eyes blank. A huge pile of peeled cedar posts, his new suit—it had all gone down his brother-in-law's throat!

Sandy glanced at the stiffness in his wife's back, then at the misery in John's face. "What is it?"

"You took the money from the drawer, Sandy?" She didn't even turn around.

Her husband sat down slowly. "I'm afraid so. Samson came by and . . ." he stopped and looked around.

"It was John's."

"John's?" Sandy looked at him. "Yours?"

Still not saying a word, John nodded.

The man hid his face in his hands. After a while he looked up. "I'm awfully sorry, John," he said huskily. "I wish I could tell you how sorry I am." He hit his fist against the table. "Oh, if only I could quit this whiskey business. I'm sorry. So sorry."

They all sat there helplessly, and after a while they ate. "I'll make it up to you somehow," Sandy promised him as he left for work at a logging camp.

As he walked to school John was dubious. Sandy wouldn't ever have enough to spare anything for him. That fifteen dollars was gone forever, he was sure. And it was whiskey that had done it. Well, no question about it. John wasn't ever going to touch the stuff again. The fellows at work had let him have a sip now and then, and he was acquiring the taste, but if whiskey could turn Sandy into a thief and make him mean to Flora at times—no thank you.

John went back to peeling cedar posts, and somehow he managed to finish out the school term. And Sandy did make it up to him. Grinning all across his whiskered face, he announced one day, "I've got you something better. Now you'll make some *real* cash." It was a summer job in a nearby logging camp as cook's devil. The boy was too young to crosscut or pile logs, but his brother-in-law had talked the cook into taking on help.

By the beginning of the fall term of school, John was getting to know people. In fact, a Mr. McEwen, a retired Member of Parliament, came over one evening and offered to give him some help.

"But I can't take something for nothing," John protested when McEwen made his offer.

"It wouldn't be for nothing," the man insisted. "My wife and I expect great things from you, and we want you to get the best start possible. Come along, now. We have an errand to run."

The errand was to town, and there they fitted John with clothes, even a hat. His long-postponed suit was finally a reality.

John insisted on doing chores for the couple, but even so, he realized that it didn't begin to cover what they were spending on him. He resolved to find work that would make him financially independent, yet still let him continue with his schooling. By summer he had found the first thing. A dealer in cattle needed someone to drive a herd to Gore Bay for shipment across the lake.

"Gore Bay!" he told his sister. "Do you know what that means? I'll get a chance to see the ships."

"So?" she questioned, refusing to get excited about it. "It's just a short-term job, John. What will you do after that?"

"Maybe I'll hire on as a crew member on one of those ships. I could sail Georgian Bay to Owen Sound, take a train to Toronto or Montreal, hire on an ocean-going vessel, and see the world," he spun out, only half joking.

Flora swung around on him. "Don't you dare!"

Her brother grinned. "There probably won't be any in port anyway." He pretended to sigh. But he was thinking about it seriously when he started out with the cattle. His boyhood fantasy had been to be a sailor and go off to the ends of the earth. "Probably to get away from Father," he told himself. And speaking of his father, he wondered what the deacon had said the morning he found his son had disappeared again. No telling. At least he hadn't been able to follow him this time, and surely now it was too late. He hoped his mother was doing OK. Kicking at a rock in the road, he put his past behind him.

At Gore Bay, after receiving his pay, John headed for the wharf. He just had to see whether a boat was there. Suddenly he felt that it was his only chance for great adventure. Shoving his hands deep into his pockets, he chose a back street and set out. He could almost feel the dampness in the breeze blowing off the bay, and he imagined the sensation of the waves rolling under the deck his feet walked on.

"Heck! What are *you* doing here?"

John whirled around. The voice was familiar, but he couldn't place it.

"Bob! Is it really you, or am I imagining things?"

"Really me," laughed Bob Bryan of John's chokecherry days.

"But what are you doing here?" Unconsciously John echoed

Bob's question.

"I've run away from home, Heck . . ."

"No Heck any more, Bob. It's John now."

"John, then. I've run away from home. I'm on my own now."

Suddenly a wave of enthusiasm washed over McEachern. "Come with me, Bob," he suggested, his eyes almost dancing. "We'll board a ship and see the world!"

His friend scuffed his shoe in the dirt for a moment. Then he shook his head slowly. "I can't do it, John. I've signed up for work with a gang of men going to Meldrum Bay logging camp. I need to work for months yet." He looked at his friend pleadingly. "Come, John. Go logging with me. Then I'll go with you, and we'll sail the seas and see the world together."

Turning, John headed for the wharf again, but Bob kept step with him. "You don't want to go alone, man. Give me a year, and then I'll stick with you wherever you want to go."

A ship was in harbor. Sailors were already loosening the ropes, scurrying around with all the last-minute preparations for sailing. John approached the gangplank, his friend still pleading at his side.

On one hand, here was his ship, maybe the chance of his lifetime. On the other hand, it would be fun to work with his friend. They could go sailing later. Finally, as the sailors seemed ready to hoist the gangplank, John made up his mind. "It's a deal, Bob. We'll be loggers first."

It was a decision that would change his whole outlook, and shape for him a very different life from that which he had planned or ever dreamed of. But he didn't know that. All he knew was that Meldrum Bay was even farther from home than Tehkummah or Gore Bay, and no one would think of reaching him there. Except Flora. He would send word to her.

27

4

Grand Manitoulin was heavily wooded with pine, cedar, birch, some maple, and even a bit of wild apple. Logging companies were making great inroads into the forests. They could sell the logs for lumber, or for cedar posts and fence rails. Manitoulin farms are still edged with rail fences. Almost every bay had a port for lumber loading, and Meldrum Bay had one of the main docks. Its picturesque village had the usual attractions for loggers, but it had more than that. Big oil-burning lamps at the lighthouse led the ships through the deep-blue waters of Mississagi Strait. It was even said that the Mississagi Strait was where La Salle, the French explorer, had his ship *Griffon* sink during a storm way back in 1679.

The two young men felt as though they were already seeing a little of the big world the afternoon they walked into Meldrum Bay so John could sign on for work with the logging company.

"It's not the easiest job," Bob explained as they checked into camp and stowed their things in the bunkhouse. "We're cook's devils, which means . . ."

"I know," John interrupted dryly. "The lowest of the low. I've been there."

His friend laughed. "Then you are broken in already."

They had to get the teamsters up at 4:00 A.M., breakfast them, and get them out on the sleigh road early. Then they washed the dishes and cleaned up the camp kitchen just in time to start the next meal.

At least the two young men did not go hungry. Logging camps had lots to eat. John didn't just stretch out a bit. He fattened up like a young billy goat; the gnawing mouse in his stomach finally put to a permanent rest.

It wasn't just the food. The clean, fresh air, the wind off the bay, the scent of freshly cut wood . . . John thrived on it. The crew bosses soon promoted him to cutting new logs with the others. He was hard at it one day, when he looked up at the sound of a voice.

"John McEachern, I believe?"

The young man felt like rubbing his eyes. If they weren't deceiving him, it was his book salesman from his cornfield days at Mr. Williams' farm.

It seemed stupid, but all he could say was "How did you find me?"

Mr. Carr laughed. "Coincidence, John. I'm canvassing all the logging camps, and I always ask the bookkeeper to let me see the loggers' names. I couldn't believe it myself when I saw yours there."

"You remembered after all this time?"

"Looks like it, doesn't it?" The man smiled.

Glancing around, John saw the boss standing nearby, watching them. Mr. Carr noticed, too. "I've got permission to show you my books, but not for long." He raised his voice so the other loggers could hear and hurried through a canvass. No one dared take time to look at the books or fill out the order blank, as they were being timed, so Mr. Carr left, still cheerful, saying that he would see them later some time.

Sunday, Bob and John had promised to visit a neighboring logging camp, and they left as soon as they could get off. To their great surprise, Carr was there also, taking orders for books. Also, as it was Sunday, he had received permission to preach to the men.

The meeting took place in the bunkhouse. Most of the loggers were lounging around, aimlessly loafing, spitting tobacco juice, and telling yarns. Carr made himself at home.

Having grown up as a sheepherder in Montana, he was used to men of the outdoors. He had a way with words, and as John listened, he felt a stirring inside, almost like a lump in his throat or a flutter of nerves. It was totally unfamiliar to him, and he wasn't quite sure what to do with it.

When the talk ended, he drew Bob aside. "Let's take Carr back to our camp for the night."

"Sure. Why not?" Bob agreed.

But things didn't go as expected.

The men drifted back into camp drunk. They looked Carr over and sized him up much in the same way as McDonald had. "You looking for work, fellow?" they asked. When Carr started to explain they gruffly interrupted with "There's no room here for men like you."

"We'll find a place for you to sleep," the boys assured him.

But the salesman turned and walked out of camp. John followed him.

"Don't go out into the night, please," he begged. "You'll get lost. There are wild animals too. It's really dangerous."

Carr turned around and put his hand on the young man's shoulder. "It's like this with me, John," he said earnestly. "If my God sees fit, I'd just as soon lie down and die in these woods. If God wants me to keep working for Him, His angels are with me, and I'm afraid of nothing. In my Christian work I never stay where I'm unwelcome. The Lord has some place for me to stay tonight, but it's not here."

John walked with him to where the road divided, and pointed the way that led to a little settlement. "It's not far, now. Just under a mile."

"Thank you, John. But before I go, let's have a word of prayer." And to John's surprise, Mr. Carr knelt right there beside the road. Feeling awkward, but not knowing what else to do, John knelt also. He had never heard anyone pray like the salesman did. It was no preacher vocabulary. Only a man talking with his Friend, pleading for a special blessing for the loggers, and particularly for John. Heaven seemed pretty close with a fellow like this.

"Mr. Carr," he said when they were back on their feet, "is there any way I can get a copy of your book before you return?"

"We don't deliver before pay time, but I can have your book sent by mail."

The man lit a match, John counted out the cash charge in its feeble light, and they parted in the darkness.

Ten days later a package arrived. Mail came to the camp only once a week. "We're saving it until Sunday," John told Bob positively. "It'll give us something to look forward to." So all week they sawed and chopped and lifted logs and thought of the book they were going to read. As soon as Sunday morning chores were over, the two boys climbed into the top bunk and unwrapped the book. "*The Coming King.*" John read the title out loud. "Hmmm. How are we going to do this? How about taking turns reading out loud?"

"Suits, me," said Bob.

"Good. You start." John laid back and put his hands behind his head.

"You're a lazy bum, but I suppose I will." Bob began with a good will but found the book affected him strangely. His voice kept faltering to a stop. Tears gathered in his eyes. Finally John reached over and took the book. Funny thing, it affected him the same way. Bob read and cried. John read and cried. Then Bob read again, and cried again. Finally John took his turn until he was too choked up to go on. The book was no treatise about hellfire, said nothing about the wicked whom John had been told would be roasted a thousand years on one side, then turned for a thousand on the other, ad infinitum. Instead, they found a merciful God, a loving Saviour, a beautiful heaven from which the Lord would descend and gather His people. And His people were not only a few choice predestined saints—they were simply those people who had believed and accepted Christ as a personal Saviour.

"I never thought God could be like that," John explained, wiping his eyes on his shirt sleeve. All I knew about Him was

31

that He wanted people to suffer. I hated Him." He thought for a moment. "I think I believed He was like my father," he confessed. "Always looking for an excuse to punish me."

"If this book is right," Bob reflected, "I wouldn't mind getting to know God."

Both boys lay there quietly for a while, thinking private thoughts. "It makes sense," John added, breaking the silence, "to *destroy* all the things that are bad and the people who hang on to them. I never could see any good reason for torturing people continuously. That just keeps sin around, continues the fight between God and sinful people. I mean, if I were burning for years on end, I'd have a lot of hateful things to say to and about God."

"Carr must believe the same as this book." Bob sat up and promptly bumped his head on the low ceiling of the bunkhouse. "Ow!" He rubbed his head, and John laughed up at him.

"Jog your brain a bit after all this hard thinking!" He sobered up. "You're right, though. Carr deserves respect, and the way he acts, I think God is decent after all."

Bob had been watching for his chance. Seeing John losing himself in thought again, he swiftly reached over and started rolling him off the bunk.

"Hey!" John yelled. "What do you think you're doing?" He grabbed for anything with which to stabilize himself. All he found was the blanket, and it simply rolled along with him. Bob got tangled in it for a moment, and it was a toss-up who would land on the floor. In the end no one did, but the bunk looked as if it had been through a major disaster.

"So, who cares?" Bob said, looking up after descending the ladder safely. "It'll sleep just as well. C'mon. We've got to get out for a while."

5

Wintertime came. Snow blanketed the forest, and the mornings were icy. Even so, the logging camp didn't slow down at all. It seemed as though they got up in the middle of the night, John complained to himself, and worked until after dark. Still, the holidays were coming up. All the men received time off at Christmas, and that created a problem for him. What was he going to do? For a while he considered going to Tehkummah and spending the time with Flora and Sandy, but strangely enough, for the first time he felt homesick. Perhaps, he thought to himself, his mother was as lonely as he was. And, too, his parents didn't even know where he was. His sister had kept his whereabouts a secret. If anything had happened, to his mother or father, he wouldn't even know about it. At last, when some of the men began leaving for the holiday, John decided he too just had to go home, and set out by himself.

It was a long way, and he knew no place where he could stay. So he walked all day, then all night, and arrived home in the early morning. All the time he was visualizing how things would be. "I'll just burst in and surprise them," he said to himself. Pulling the latch string, he opened the door. His father and mother were there alone and still in bed.

His mother, so thin and white! His father, how gray! It was like a fist slamming into his stomach. He had never thought about their changing—had always imagined their staying the same. But time had gone on writing its tale in the lines of their faces, in the changing of color in their hair, the fading of their eyes. When his mother got up to make breakfast, John's emotions became too strong for him to stay inside.

"I'll go out and look around a bit, Mother," he said.

But once outside, there wasn't that much to see. Finally he went up to his old haunt on the hill, sat down in the cold, and thought and thought. A stiff breeze came up and ruffled his hair, blowing moisture into his eyes and making him shiver. Still he remained there, his life flowing before his inner sight. When he stood at last, he had made a decision. As he returned to the house, his step felt lighter, his appetite had returned.

At the table John answered his mother's eager questions rather absently, telling her—and his father listened—about his school days at Flora's and about his life at the logging camp. He was still hungry when the food was gone, but he knew there was no more here.

"Thank you for the breakfast, Mother. I've got some errands to run, but I'll be back soon."

The first thing he wanted was to find a furniture dealer. His mother had never had a chair. John hadn't noticed that before. Now the cabin looked like a shanty, and the beds were straw ticks, refilled once in a while when fresh straw was available.

He didn't have much money with him, but once he found the dealer, he bargained for a rocking chair. It was his first Christmas present to his mother. If he was going to get anything else, he would have to go back to earning money. That he had known from the start. But in the meantime, someone was going to have to take care of his parents. He racked his brain on the way back home. Summers he would stay home, but work the rest of the year. Maybe . . .

Visiting an unmarried sister, he told her, "Euphemia, I need help." She considered things carefully as he explained his plans.

"I guess I'll go, John," she said finally.

Once she arrived, he went back to finish the winter at the logging camp, his plans for sailing around the world or for finishing school postponed. He had his life ahead of him, but his parents didn't, and he wanted to care for them at whatever cost.

Summers he spent planting, harvesting, and working for neighbor farmers. Things really began to change at the McEachern place. The first summer he moved his parents to a more respectable house. Still in his teens, John started making payments on a newer place with better accommodations and land. Unselfishly he put all he had into accomplishing what he had determined to do that cold morning up on the bluff.

There were harder things than work, though. Deacon McEachern hadn't changed, and though John was grown now, the two still had disagreements. Sometimes they were quite heated. John found himself caught in a quandary. His father was still the head of the house—or was he? It was John's money, John's work, John's initiative and drive that was caring for them now, and he didn't see why that should awaken opposition in his father. He couldn't understand that every improvement had an implied criticism in it of the old man's ways.

It was always, "The corn won't grow as well there," after John had planted a crop. Or "It's a fool notion you have to be buying all that new-fangled equipment" after John had just invested hard-earned money in an iron stove that would also help heat the house. Biting his tongue, John tried to keep silent.

One day it came to a head in a way neither of them had expected. Mrs. McEachern had said something or done something—John never found out which—to arouse her husband's wrath. John came in the door just as the deacon raised his hand to strike her.

"Stop it!" the son shouted. "Don't you dare touch her!"

The deacon hesitated, his arm still lifted. His eyes scornful, he slowly turned to look at John.

"If you ever do that again," John said coldly, his voice bitter and heavy, "I'll wipe up the earth with your raw hide!"

The deacon lowered his arm in amazement and turned on

him, but suddenly he stopped. The old man faced a young logger, muscles iron-hard from constant sawing and chopping and lifting. Suddenly he saw, not the teenage Heck his mind still insisted on, but a grown man, fire flashing from his flinty eyes, hands clenched, ready to lash out. The deacon turned away sulkily, mumbling something under his breath. Then he left the room.

John stood there astonished at himself, feeling a little shaky. He had actually, finally, dared to come between his mother and his overbearing father. And why hadn't he done it long ago?

She crossed the room in one swift movement and put her arms around her tall son. Neither of them said a word. Both had tears in their eyes. John rocked her back and forth for a moment, as though to tell her she had nothing more to fear. And he was right. The deacon never raised an arm to strike his wife again. He never dared.

John was thoughtful as he walked off to the logging camp a few days later, his emotions still stirred by what had happened between him and his father. The confrontation had left him feeling stronger. He felt himself free of his lifelong fear of his father. And he still experienced a joy from shielding his mother. But—strange. What he felt for his father now, what was it? Pity? Hate? "I think I despise him," he told himself, and he felt guilty. That wasn't right either. He struggled with his feelings a little more as his long strides carried him toward the overnight stop at Flora's. Now he always went that way.

Camp seemed rather empty that second winter. Bob had not come back, and John had to go it alone, had to measure himself against more experienced men. Somehow he had to gain their respect while trying to be a Christian. Trouble is, he thought, I'm not sure how a Christian acts.

Flora always packed a Bible into his turkey. One day it fell out. "What do you know!" the logger next to him exclaimed. "Mac has a Bible!" Picking up a bootjack, he threw it at John, purposely aiming high so it would just skim his head.

John ignored the man completely. It had just occurred to him that maybe by reading the Bible he could get some of his questions answered. At least he would give it a try. But he leafed through it aimlessly, not sure how to go about it or where to start. Finally he repacked it and decided he would think about it while he was working in the morning.

The morning had another surprise for him. He was whistling as he collected his tools, joking with some of the men, when he felt a funny sensation as though someone else had entered the toolshed. Glancing around, he saw Mr. Carr, an expectant smile spread over his face.

"You've got to quit doing this to me." John smiled back as he went over to shake his friend's hand.

"Thought you might need another book," the salesman said, returning the handshake. "How did you like the first one?"

Briefly John told him of his experience with Bob, omitting some of the details, such as the crying sessions. "It made us feel like God might really care," he explained. The men were trooping off to work, and John knew he should join them. "Can you stay until tonight? I'd really like to have another book if it's anything like the first one."

John's book came in the mail again. *Daniel and the Revelation* it was called, and he couldn't wait to get into it. Every night by candlelight he read a little, and on Sundays he spent hours at a time absorbing it. He liked the stories about Daniel, presented in a new way altogether. The world history and the chronological prophecies and their fulfillment fascinated him. The thought that the end of the world might be soon, no longer conjured up pictures of hell and torment for him. Now it meant that the heavenly King might come to take His own.

Tremendously impressed by Daniel's integrity, his faithfulness to what he knew to be right, John read on and on. He felt good now about what he was doing for his parents. Now he began thinking of other things. While he didn't drink liquor as the other men did, the book was making him feel uncomfortable about his language. Deciding to stop his swearing, for six weeks he kept close track of what he said.

Once that was cleaned up, he decided he needed to change other things in his life. Maybe he should do as his mother and kneel for prayer. *That* would take some courage, because the men would see him. Feeling as if he were approaching the fiery furnace, John knelt for prayer that night. He could hear the remarks behind him, and his ears turned a little red.

"Mac's got religion for sure. Look at him!"

"McEachern's repenting of his sins. Wonder what he did this time!"

Ignoring them, John continued to pray. Before he climbed into his bunk, however, one huge lumberman ambled up to him and said, "It's OK, fellow. Anyone bothers you, just call on me." With a wink he ambled off again. As John watched him go, he felt a surge of gratitude welling up inside him.

Trouble was, the praying didn't solve things. Got little devils jumping in my skull, he often thought as he pulled on the saw. Pictures of his father rose up to plague him. "Got hate in your heart," a voice accused. "Your father's so religious, and look what he does to your mother," another one laughed. "Religion is just a way of scaring people on Sunday so they can go take it out on Monday by scaring others." That last voice was an echo of years of his own thinking. He recognized it but couldn't get rid of it.

Some days, looking up at the tall trees all around him, smelling the fragrance of fresh-cut wood, it was easy to believe in the God of Mr. Carr. Other days he was in an agony of soul, convicted of his own sins, sure he was predestined to burn in hell just as his father had told him through all the years. On those days he wanted to curse and swear and throw things, for he found no relief at all.

One night, in desperation, he went out to walk the sleigh road packed with snow. Looking up at the clear, starry sky, he begged, "Please, God, show me if I'm to be saved or lost. I can't go on this way." He confessed all the things he could think of, then repeated his cry, "Please, God."

Returning to his bunk, he climbed in and fell asleep. Then he dreamed. At first it was a nightmarish experience. He was in a deep mire, caught, but struggling. No matter how hard he tried to escape, he kept sinking. He kept trying to climb out, but the banks were so steep he couldn't get a toehold. A limb here and there seemed to offer a means of help, but every time he got hold of a limb and pulled himself up a little, he would encounter the face of an awful beast, foaming at the mouth and ready to devour him. Reaching the end of his endurance, he was slipping back for what seemed the last time, when he happened to glance toward the top of the precipice. There, leaning over him, was a beautiful celestial being who extended his hand down to John's and lifted him up. No need for any toehold. The place he now entered was wrapped in glory, and he heard the music of heaven.

"Wake up," said a rough voice. A hand was shaking him. "Wake up."

"What is it?" John asked, bewildered and not entirely sure where he was.

"You're tossing and turning and shaking the whole place," the other man complained. "Settle down, will you? I want some sleep."

John couldn't go back to sleep for a long time. The whole atmosphere of that heavenly place seemed to be all around him, as though heaven itself had come to earth. The conflict was gone from his heart. He felt the assurance of acceptance.

Finally he fell asleep, and someone had to shake him in the morning when he didn't wake up on time. He went off to the woods more cheerful than he had been in a long time and went to chopping wood so vigorously that the other men began to tease him.

"Mac must have found a girl."

"Yeah, man. Look at him with that ax! He thinks he's eight feet tall!"

John just grinned and went on working.

He read his books carefully now and started in on his Bible, looking for ways to be a Christian. John felt a close relationship to the man who had sold him the books, and even though he didn't see him often, he tried to learn to live life the way the book salesman did.

The day came when John became convinced that he should start observing the Sabbath. Both of his books mentioned it, and checking the references in his Bible, he was sure they were right. Besides this, he remembered now that Mr. Carr's Sunday was Saturday, and while he hadn't put much importance on it before, it had been such an unusual thing that he had remembered it.

Logging camp knew no Sabbath. Sunday was just a day off, and the men generally spent it in most any way except a religious one. They played cards, gambled, went off and got drunk, started fights, visited places with less than a good reputation, and smashed a few things once in a while.

The other days of the week were busy ones. The company could not spare a logger on any other day. So when John came up to the foreman to explain what he wanted, the foreman was stumped.

"You're a good logger, John. You stay sober, and you do your work well. But Saturdays off?" He scratched his head, then stroked his whiskers. "I hardly know what to tell you."

Obviously the man was turning it over in his mind, so John waited patiently, praying that he would be able to stay on. He didn't know of any other way he could keep earning money to care for himself and his parents, and if he lost his job here, what would he do? His family was dependent on him now.

The foreman shook his head slowly. "No way I can do it, John. There's just no way. It's absolutely impossible."

John's heart sank to his shoes. Big as he was, he felt like crying.

"You know how it is, John. I like you and all, but give you a whole day off—it would create chaos. You can't work on

Sunday all alone, and I can't give all the fellows Saturday off. I'll just have to look for someone to take your place." He looked at him intently. "You sure you're set on this?"

John just nodded.

"Well I wish you luck, fellow. But curses on that man who sold you those books. He's just stolen a good logger from me!"

After packing up and saying his goodbyes, John started home with a heavy heart. It was a long time until he could do the plowing and planting, and besides, he needed money to get them through the coming year. What was he going to do? He racked his brain, but he just couldn't think of anything that would fill in those weeks and still leave him free for his spring plowing.

"Why did You let this happen, God?" he prayed as he walked. But the memory of his dream came to him, and he could see again the beautiful face bent over him in love, offering a helping hand. His heart lifted, and he quickened his pace. Something would turn up for sure.

6

A familiar figure sat on the porch of his house when he finally arrived home. John felt as though the experience had happened to him several times before.

"Mr. Carr," he greeted him with a shake of the head, "you always show up when I least expect you."

The man just grinned and held out his hand. "Heard you were out of a job, and I had an idea you might need something to do."

"How did you find out so fast?"

"Word gets around. I've been working the logging camps for a while, now."

"Well, come in and let's talk about it." The two men went inside. "Mother, we have company," John called out as he shut the door behind him.

"You're company too, this time of year, John," his mother answered as she appeared from another room.

"I know," her son said ruefully. "But it seems I have no choice."

While Mrs. McEachern fixed some supper, John talked things over with Carr.

"There's a lot of territory out here, John," the book salesman began. "I haven't begun to cover it. You could learn to sell books with me for a while, then go it on your own."

It was a totally new idea. The young man sat back and considered it. Certainly it would be something different from logging, but it could be a way to learn and earn money at the same time. He would really welcome the chance to spend time with Mr. Carr. To be with someone who did not swear, who not only shared his faith in God but could help make it stronger . . . He looked sideways at his father, who was sitting across the room, pretending not to listen. Although he was almost ashamed to admit it to himself, in some ways he would welcome not having to live in the same house with the deacon these additional months.

On impulse he leaned across the space on the sofa. "I'll do it, Mr. Carr! There's really no reason why I shouldn't, and I do need the money."

The man held out his hand. "It's a deal then, John. You won't regret it."

The next day, the two men left, traveling on a dogsled, pulled by a team of two huge dogs, harnessed like horses. The sled had a barrel fixed to it. Inside the barrel were books and things needed for travel. The men sat on top of the barrel, with staves nailed on at the back to lean against.

John waved to his mother who stood at the door. Mr. Carr took up the slack in the reins, and called out, "Gee, Hoo," and Buck and Jack took off just like a regular team of horses.

"Can't believe how fast they go," John said with a grin, feeling the road hard and smooth under them, the scenery falling away behind them.

"Roads are icy and frozen. Makes it easy," Carr answered laconically.

"Where are we headed?"

"Little Current, at the end of the island."

"But aren't there some lakes on the way?" John felt a little concerned.

The salesman just shrugged. "Frozen over."

John continued to worry. The sled load was heavy—two dogs, two men, a barrel of books, boots, and baggage. It wasn't the coldest time of winter, and by now air holes would pocket the lake ice. If the sled dropped into an air hole . . . He shuddered.

The dogs approached Lake Mindemoya without hesitation. John could see far out to the island, shaped like an old woman, for which the lake was named. Briefly he thought of the Algonquin legend of the Indian chief who had kicked his wife over a cliff for spoiling his brew, and how she had landed in the lake. But in another instant he was gripping his barrel staves and holding his breath.

"It's OK, John," Mr. Carr assured him. "God is with us."

But McEachern hung on until they were safely across and onto the isthmus.

At midnight, when they came to the other lake, Manitou, things were different. The lake had a glare in the moonlight—just like that of open water. In fact, John could see where the water had come above the ice, and in the 30° below zero weather had frozen over again.

"Surely we won't try that lake," he commented.

"No," Carr said reluctantly, halting the dogs. "I guess we'd better not try it at nighttime."

"But where in the world will we stay? It's already midnight."

"Oh, don't worry about that. The Lord has a place for us."

Glancing around him at the empty landscape, John felt a little skeptical, but the older man had spotted a house up on a distant hillside.

"See that house there, John?"

"Yes."

"We're going to stay there."

"But, I'm sure they're already in bed."

"It won't matter." Carr clucked to the dogs and, pulling them in a tight half circle, they headed away from the lake and toward the hill. It was quite a distance, and once there, the hill was pretty steep. John wasn't real sure about all this, but Mr. Carr was in charge, so he didn't say anything. Finally they got to the house. Stepping out of the sled, the salesman walked right up to the door and knocked vigorously.

"Who's there?" bellowed a voice into the night.

"It's me," Carr answered in such a familiar tone that the man assumed it was a neighbor and came down to open the door. He looked so funny, standing there in his nightshirt, gaping at them, that John almost chuckled.

"We're traveling with a sled," Carr explained reasonably, "and the roads are best for that this time of year. But we were wondering whether to try crossing Manitou Lake to get to Little Current."

The man looked worried. "I wouldn't try to cross that lake at night!"

"Well, how do we get around it?"

The man looked even more disturbed. "You'd better just turn in and wait here till morning," he decided finally. "You two unhitch the dogs while I get dressed." He returned in a few minutes, took the dogs to his barn, and fed them a good meal of raw meat. In the meantime, his wife got up and prepared hot drinks for the men. After a friendly Canadian chat over the drink, they all went off to bed. Before he fell asleep, John found himself thinking that he was learning faster than he expected.

They had prayer with the couple in the early morning, then set out to cross the lake. The top ice was slippery enough for the sled to glide easily and the dogs' feet had good traction. John was beginning to feel confident enough to loosen his tight grip on the sled when suddenly he spotted a huge crack in the ice dead ahead. "Look out!" he yelled at the top of his voice. The crack was enormous. The ice had receded, and the crack seemed to stretch the whole length of the lake. Mr. Carr reined in the dogs.

"How do we get around that?" John called out. "The lake must be fifteen miles long."

"Can't afford to waste time going around," the salesman decided. "Let's go over."

John never figured out whether that was faith or presumption, but at the moment he didn't have any time to think about it. Carr put the whip to the dogs, and they reached such momentum that they couldn't have stopped if they had wanted to. Over the crack they hurtled, and soon the sled, barrel, books, men, and all were safely on the other side, headed for the village of Little Current. John didn't relax his hold on the sled until he was sure they had solid ground under them.

Little Current was only a settlement, but it fascinated John. In the first place, only a hundred-yard passage separated the mainland of Ontario and the island of Grand Manitoulin. The water of Lake Huron's North Channel funnels itself back and forth through that passage. The town was large enough to have a little Methodist church, and the people were gathering for an afternoon meeting when the two men arrived.

Carr always seemed to know just what to do. John watched him carefully, but never could imitate him exactly or figure out what it was—for that matter—that made people take to him immediately. The churchgoers asked him to take part in their services almost before the two men could climb out of their sled. As Carr spoke, McEachern thought about the other things he did easily. The book salesman had told him stories of delivering babies, administering herbs, manipulating bones— seemed as though he could play doctor on the side, too.

It was no problem finding a place to sleep that night. In fact, they could pick and choose among the offers. But the next morning, it was time for John to get to work. He had his own copy of *The Coming King.* Carr explained that he was to show the book in every home he went to. Then people would sign their names and addresses for one like it to be delivered at a later date. It sounded simple, but John wasn't entirely convinced. In the back of his mind lingered the picture of McDonald leaning on his hoe and telling Carr what he thought of people who were too lazy to plant corn.

They went to the edge of town. "John, you take this road into Manitoulin," Carr said, "and I'll take the other road down toward Sheguiandah."

Left on his own, McEachern suddenly felt shaky. Longingly he thought of the timber crews that had always gone together to saw and chop in the forests. If only he could go back to having an ax in his hand! He looked down the road at the first house. Just a house. Doors, windows, a gate. What was he scared of? Squaring his shoulders, he marched up the road to the house, not daring even to stop and wonder what he would say if anyone should open the door.

Fortunately he didn't have time to wonder. A woman came to the door and kindly invited him in. John laid his book on his knees, and trembling inwardly, started to tell her about it. In a few minutes he forgot all about being nervous. He remembered vividly that Sunday when he and Bob had first discovered a God of love, and he timidly told her that reading the book had led him to Jesus.

"Oh, if that book is what has helped you, young man," she exclaimed, "then I want it for my boys. I want them to be Christians." She found a pen and wrote her name down for the book.

McEachern felt as though he had grown wings on his feet as he walked out of the house. "An order the first time," he exulted. "Maybe I *can* do it after all!" Encouraged, he continued on down the road, talking in his inexperienced, awkward way, but with sincerity shining through all he said.

"Excellent, John!" Mr. Carr told him happily. "I knew you could do it!"

The two men worked on together for a few days, then Carr decided it was time for him to go on his own. John agreed. He wasn't afraid any more, and they could cover more territory if each went a different way.

"See you in a few weeks," the older man called as he climbed back into the sled. "Gee, Hoo, Buck, Jack!"

John watched them until they were lost in the white stillness. Then he tucked his book under his arm and returned to his door-knocking. In time he struck difficult territory. The individuals there had no desire to learn anything about any religion, and many of them were indifferent to people, as well. Try as he did, he could not convince them to order anything.

47

Worse than that, they seldom invited him to share a meal or stay for the night.

One day he felt he had reached the bottom of his barrel. He had seventy-five cents in his pocket—had carried it for many weeks, in fact. Dinner had been light, and he had had no supper. Night was coming on, and he was far out in the country. The houses were few and far apart, and sometimes the wind carried the sound of a wolf howl. Shivering, he knocked at the door of an isolated house. A man opened the door a crack.

"I was wondering if it would be possible for me to get a place to stay for the night," John began.

"There's a village down there a few miles," the man grunted. "Strangers like you can go to hotels." The door shut.

Discouraged, John started off again. A mile down the road he tried a farmhouse. "I'm sure you can get a place in the village for only 50 cents," the farmer told him, and again the door closed in his face.

It was snowing, and the wind blew the cold flakes against his cheeks. By now it was nine o'clock at night. "What can I do?" John asked himself desperately. "I can't sleep out in the cold." Finally he wandered back to the village. Finding the hotel, he pushed the door open and went into the lobby. For a few minutes he just stood there, rubbing his hands and trying to absorb some of the warmth. Then, at last, he went to the clerk.

The man shoved a book over the counter. "Sign here, please."

John signed.

"That'll be 75 cents."

"They told me it was 50," McEachern protested, almost stammering.

"Seventy-five." The clerk didn't even explain. Reluctantly, John reached into his pocket and took out his money. It was all he had. The clerk showed him up to a cold room where he shivered the whole night through, waiting for dawn. Hungry and discouraged, he thought again of his ax and saw and of the friendly banter of the logging camp, but there was no turning back.

A chilly dawn finally broke through the windows, and John left the hotel almost gladly. He started out for the territory he had tried to break into the night before, but he didn't have very high expectations. People sure weren't friendly around here. It had snowed four to six inches during the night. The snow was light and fluffy, giving way under his feet wherever he stepped. In fact, he found himself peering closely at it, trying to find the sleigh road buried under it. There was just one street in the village, and he followed it, wondering to himself why the Lord had left him there alone. Very alone.

Lost in thought, he forgot to watch where he was going. Suddenly his foot hit ice, and he slipped, losing his balance. After sliding around for a few minutes, he finally managed to regain his balance. He pulled his shoe out of the snow and saw something strange on the end of it. Carefully he leaned over to look more closely. "Well, of all things!" he said out loud. Taking the paper carefully between his fingers, he turned it over. It was a five-dollar bill. How'd that get into the snow? he wondered, then stood there thoughtfully considering the situation.

"Somebody must have lost this," he decided. "I'd better report it." Turning, he walked back down to the post office and waited there until the postmaster came and opened the wicket. The official had a white beard, giving him a distinct resemblance to Moses.

"I found this in the snow," John explained, holding up the bill. "It was right at the end of the road as you start getting into the country. Maybe it belongs to somebody."

The man was already shaking his head. "No one has reported losing anything, and there's no way of finding out who—if anyone around here—is missing that money." He smiled through his white beard. "My lad, that is just your good luck. Nobody will ever expect to find money after last night's snowstorm. Just you put that in your pocket. It's yours."

John didn't argue. The postmaster represented the authority of the government of Canada, and his word was law. Suddenly quite cheerful, John marched out of the post office. He looked up briefly, glanced around, then bowed his head. "You knew, didn't You? You were watching the whole time. Thanks for helping me."

As he sat in the restaurant waiting for his breakfast he decided that his guardian angel must have hidden the money in the snow, then tripped him at just the right moment. The idea made him smile.

And he was still smiling when he walked out warm and with his stomach full, and that smile must have made a difference. The first house he went to gave him an order. Someone else invited him to dinner, and the next two nights people took him in and gave him a place to stay.

Things were never quite that tough again. On weekends, when he met with Mr. Carr to talk things over, they determined the new territory he would cover. By the end of the winter, John had taken orders for many books, which he promised to deliver after harvest in the fall.

"Guess you'll be headed home now, John."

"It's time," McEachern agreed. "I've got to get the fields plowed and planted."

"Fine. But before you go, I think it would be a good idea for you to make plans to attend the camp meeting in August."

"Camp meeting?" John was curious.

"It's a week of meetings," the older man explained. "They are held every year. This year it's going to be in London, Ontario. There will be a large tent for general assemblies, which are held several times every day. Youth and children gather in smaller tents. The people stay in dormitorylike tents or smaller ones for individual families."

John listened eagerly. "The people who go there are Christians?" he asked.

"Oh, yes," Mr. Carr assured him. "There are other meetings, too. Bible studies, helpful health lectures, talks about life's problems. They serve meals regularly . . ."

John started his long walk home, but he had plenty to think about. Somehow he would have to get his work done by August so he could . . .

7

Spring thaw came at last. John worked extra hard in the fields at home, and the time went surprisingly fast. He had so much to do and so much to think about that August caught him almost by surprise. By now his parents were so used to his comings and goings that when he explained matter-of-factly where he was off to, it hardly made a stir. Although John thought he saw a spark of interest in his father's eyes, he was afraid to follow through with it. They seldom spoke seriously or personally to each other these days. Almost as if they were strangers living in the same house.

"I try to be polite and kind to him," John had explained to Mr. Carr one time on a long drive, "but it's like there's a wall there. Sometimes I'd like to tell him about God the way I've come to know Him, but . . ." He groped for the right words. "But it's like there's so much between us that we can't even hear each other. I used to hate him, actually," he confessed out loud for the first time. "Now I kind of feel sorry for him."

Packing his things for the trip, he just said Goodbye. It was a new kind of adventure. First he had to walk to Gore Bay. When he got on a boat there, he smiled to himself, thinking about the time he had almost made it onto another vessel, except that Bob had talked him out of it. Now he was glad he hadn't become a sailor—for more than one reason. A terrible storm came up that night as they sailed over Georgian Bay to Owen Sound. John could hardly sleep for the tossing and thrashing the boat did. At one time during the night, he was sure they were going to sink, but he felt so sick that he didn't really care. When he reached Owen Sound and saw the headlines in the papers about the shipwrecks during the storm, he marveled that he *had* arrived.

From there he rode the train to London, Ontario. During the trip he kept wondering what the visit was going to be like. Mr. Carr was the only Seventh-day Adventist he knew. If Adventists were all like him, then he fully expected to have a heavenly experience, for to him the book salesman was already in the lower ranks of the angels.

He was disappointed, of course, arriving at the campground a stranger. Mr. Carr had arranged a place for him, but he himself did not attend. His canvassing was going so well that he hated to leave. Looking for an office, John wandered through the "tent city." No one knew him, and no one seemed concerned.

"Where does one sleep?" he finally asked someone.

"Just get a tick and fill it with straw. Over there's a tent," the person told him.

Feeling lonely, he got his tick and found a tent. The meetings were good, though. The ministers and their messages were new and seemed wonderful to him. They were the first Seventh-day Adventist sermons he had ever listened to. But the loneliness hung on. For three days the time between meetings was almost painful. He watched groups of people talking happily together, and he felt left out. Friends laughed and walked around together, and he stood by the tent alone, not knowing where to go or what to do.

The third day, though, everything changed. As always, he was alone by the side of the tent.

"Young man," a soprano voice said right beside him. He almost jumped, it was so unexpected. Turning, he recognized the woman in charge of the children's tent, having peeked in once and seen her leading the songs.

"I need an organ moved across the camp to another tent. Do you suppose you could help me?"

"I'd be happy to." John smiled, hoping she didn't notice how delighted he was just to have someone to talk to.

"Then wait here, please. I'll go find some others to help." A few minutes later she reappeared with three other young fellows. "If you'll each just take a corner, please," she directed.

John took his place at one corner. It was a long way across camp to the other tent, and they had to stop often to rest. McEachern found himself liking the other young men. They joked and teased one another, but they worked hard. By the time they had deposited the organ safely in its new location, John knew their names, and they knew his. Suddenly he had some friends.

Instead of standing alone outside the tent when the meetings ended, the four of them would go to dinner together. In the afternoons they would go as a group to the youth meetings, and they all attended the baptismal classes together.

After one of the baptismal classes Elder George B. Thompson spoke personally to John about baptism. "I've been a Christian for a long time now," he told the minister, "but I didn't know about being baptized. After these classes, I can see that I should be."

The two talked quietly for a long time, and on the last Sabbath of camp meeting, John walked down into the baptismal tank. He knew now without doubt that his faults were all forgiven. His biggest desire was to do what God wanted him to do. And that wasn't really easy to figure out!

In the first place, that same Sabbath some leader hung up a map of the world and talked about missions, about sending church workers to certain foreign countries. Then the people gave a special offering for this purpose, and he realized that other people were making pledges to give at a later time. John fidgeted a little, wondering how he could help. He thought about the books he would soon be delivering and decided to pledge eight dollars.

The next thing that came up was school. Somebody got up and spoke about Lornedale Academy, and how at the school—a Seventh-day Adventist institution—a person could work his way through. The idea thrilled John. Maybe now he would have another chance to get an education.

The very day he left camp meeting he started out to deliver his books. He couldn't wait until he was finished, for then he would go home and make arrangements for his parents to be taken care of now that he would be gone for the winter. Sure that things would work out, he filled out an application for school and sent it in.

It was a beautiful autumn. The brilliant colors of the leaves matched John's mood as he traveled down the dirt roads with his packages of books. The air was crisp, cool, and clean. He could hardly get enough of it into his lungs. As he walked along he sang some of the songs he had learned at the camp meeting. Other times he reviewed in his mind some of the things he had learned, marveling at how little he really knew. He could hardly wait to get to school. There was so much more to learn!

But things had changed in the community where John had taken most of his orders. A minister there had discovered that some of his church members had actually ordered books from an Adventist book agent. The next Sunday he had climbed up into his pulpit and denounced McEachern. "Don't you take those books," he warned his congregation. "Those are Advent books. They're poison!"

Almost every home John went to had decided not to take the book after all. Day after day it was the same heartbreak. He approached his last weekend of deliveries and realized with a sinking heart that he would barely have enough money to pay the cost of the books he had ordered. And as if that weren't enough, he got a letter from conference headquarters.

John had never heard of a circular letter, of carbon paper, or stencils. He thought the circular was a personal letter to him. It reminded him that those who had pledged money at the camp meeting were to remember that their pledges were promises to the Lord, promises that should be kept, and how dreadfully wrong it would be for him to fail to honor his word.

John laid the paper and the envelope down on the table at the farmhouse where he was spending the weekend. Then slowly sitting down, he stared off into space. Not only was his heart heavy, his conscience was too. He owed God eight dollars, and he had nothing to pay with. Sabbath morning John spent walking through the woods, blind to the autumn colors now. No longer singing or whistling, he paced back and forth, praying and figuring. At last he decided to go that night to the village and try to dispose of another book or two.

As soon as the sun set, he started out, but now the weather was against him. The sky grew quickly black, and lightning flashed across the gathering darkness. The fields were dry, and the dust on the country roads was deep. John stopped walking and took stock of the situation. It was going to rain, and rain hard. For the farmers that was great. For him—well, he'd better turn back while he still could.

Even before he got back to the farm, it was so dark he could barely make out his way. To help himself stay in the road, he took to watching the bordering fences, his feet sinking into the dust of the horse-and-wagon tracks or sometimes wandering off into the dry and brown roadside grass.

Frequent flashes of lightning helped him now and then. One of them made him stop. The flash had shown a bit of green right in front of him. Green? he thought. What could be green in this drought? Stooping he began to feel around him with both hands. The dust was gritty and rough on his hands, but finally his fingers touched something different. Quickly he slipped it into his pocket.

He barely beat the storm home.

"Was wondering if you'd had the sense to come back," the farmer said with relief when McEachern shut the door behind him. "Didn't know if you knew how it is around here when it storms like this."

The first heavy spats of rain sounded on the roof. "Looked pretty bad, but I guess you'll be glad for it," John commented.

The farmer walked over to the window and stared out for a

while in silence. "Yep. Sure need it," he said finally. "It's really going to come down this time, though!"

John agreed with him, then went on up to his room and lit the kerosene lamp. Reaching into his pocket, he pulled out the object he had found along the road. It was folded up into a tight wad, so he had to work it back into shape again. To his utter astonishment, he spread out a five-dollar bill and then three ones. Exactly eight dollars! Just what he needed to pay his pledge. Now he could go home and prepare to study at that wonderful earn-and-pay-as-you-go place he had heard about at camp meeting.

But it wasn't that easy. The harvesting went slowly. Euphemia couldn't stay with his parents any longer. Toronto—near where the school was—was a long way, and he had a lot of details to settle about the trip itself. September faded into October, and November was well installed before John finally persuaded his sister Elizabeth and her husband to come and stay with his parents. Elizabeth had been living in the United States, but she and her husband had had enough of city life and agreed to come back to the island.

"It's OK now, John," she told him. "We'll stay right here and take care of everything. Get yourself off to school!"

John would walk the eighteen miles to Gore Bay—an all-night trip—and catch the morning boat to Owen Sound. He prayed with his mother and sister in the kitchen, then, deciding he really should, went into his father's room and woke him to say Goodbye.

His father turned his head on the pillow and groggily opened his eyes.

"I'm going, Father," his son told him. "Off to school, you know. I just wanted to say Goobye. Sorry to wake you up . . ." His voice trailed off at the look in the old man's eyes.

The deacon glared at him. "You just go to ————!" he spat out. "You've gone and joined up with them Advents, so that's where you are going anyway!" Then he rolled over, turning his back on his son.

The sting of the farewell burned all through the long night. John tried to shrug it off. "I should be used to it by now," he told himself bitterly, but it seemed that no amount of getting used-to helped. Later, though, on the boat, he was feeling better, and he thought of the infrequent times when his father had been a little more friendly and approachable. In fact, he remembered one time his father had actually said, "If you go through Stayner in your traveling, you might visit my brother Malcolm and take my regards." John thought about that with wavering feelings. He had never seen his uncle, and he wondered what kind of man he was. All he knew was that the man was a merchant, a successful one, and that he lived in a big, beautiful home.

Curiosity won out. John went to Stayner. Accustomed now to knocking on doors, he did not hesitate at his uncle's. A woman answered the door and invited him in. She didn't seem to object at all to taking in an unknown nephew, and she tried to make him feel at home at once.

"Your uncle is at the store, but he'll be home this evening," she said as she led him through a hall into a room that seemed almost too fancy to be in. "You just make yourself at home here," she continued. "Sit down and rest for a while. It shouldn't be too long."

John took the chair she indicated. It was a luxurious, overstuffed armchair, and when he sat down, he seemed to keep right on going. It almost scared him for a moment—he thought the bottom must be dropping out of it. Eventually he relaxed and almost fell asleep.

Uncle Malcolm was delighted to hear all about his brother and family members. He was especially happy to learn that John was on his way to school and desirous of becoming a minister. "I'll have to get the minister to come over for dinner so he can talk with you," the man beamed.

John was satisfying his curiosity. Uncle Malcolm did look a little like his father—the same rectangular face, heavy eyebrows, square hands. He was also interested in church activities, and seemed to like to talk religion, too. But he just didn't have that Calvinistic doomlike strictness to him. The man could laugh and joke and take an interest in the affairs of the big world around him.

I wonder what it's like to have a father like him, John thought with an ache of longing inside. We could have done some things together. I wonder why Father has to be so—so hell-centered and dour. I wish . . .

His stay extended into several days. The local minister, Reverend Allison, came over for dinner and immediately warmed up to John when he heard of his plans to become a minister. He thought, of course, the young man meant the Presbyterian ministry, and when in the course of the after-dinner conversation John let them all know he was a Seventh-day Adventist on his way to a Seventh-day Adventist school, the atmosphere changed a bit.

"Who in the world are Seventh-day Adventists?" his uncle asked Reverend Allison.

"I don't really know. They aren't from up here in Canada. They must be some sect from over in the United States."

Embarrassed, John squirmed a bit. Anything not acceptable in Canada was attributed to the United States, and he didn't want his religion to be thought of as odd. The men were so curious, however, that they phoned a man who had been a missionary in Japan and asked him over.

"Oh, Adventists!" the man said, once he had settled into the overstuffed chair that had given John such a scare. "I guess I do know who they are!" He glowered at John suspiciously. "Over in Japan they've been baptizing right and left. They've broken up some of our Presbyterian churches there by telling our members they have the mark of the beast because they keep Sunday."

Silence hung in the room for a few moments. Uncle Malcolm was obviously having a hard time digesting the news that he had a nephew connected with something like that described by the returned missionary. "My," he finally managed to get out, "I didn't suppose they were so prominent as to be over in Japan."

It was news to John, too, but he kept quiet, remembering the eight dollars he had sent to help mission activities open up somewhere. Now he realized that his church had quite a mission program—not just somewhere, but in a lot of places.

The missionary and the minister left shortly, and Uncle Malcolm was still thinking over what he had heard. "What kind of school is this that you're going to?" he asked.

"It's a place where a person can work for his education while he gets it," the young man explained. "I don't have any money right now, so I really need to go to a school like that."

"Well," his uncle replied, "if it's a matter of money, I'll pay your way through Knox College, and you can still be a minister. No need to worry about money."

Oh that his father were that reasonable! John felt the ache come back. "Thank you, Uncle Malcolm," he said. "You don't know how much that offer means to me, but I really can't take it. I've got to make my own way, somehow."

Uncle Malcolm was as understanding as he was reasonable, and no hard feelings existed between them. The next day John continued on his way to Lornedale Academy. Once there, he went directly to the principal's office to inquire about work, classes, and living quarters. The principal, Eugene Leland, was naturally pleased to welcome another student, but the information he had for McEachern was discouraging. Classes had begun in August, and he probably would be unable to catch up with the other students. Worse yet, the work assignments had all been made, and no more openings were available. "You could always visit classes to see for yourself what you might be getting into," Leland offered finally, not wanting to disappoint the young man entirely.

John did just that. He went with the students to meals and classes, slept in the dormitory, and rejoiced in the group devotions, worships, and Friday night vespers. The more he saw, the more he wanted to stay. The young people were

Christians and were taught by Christian teachers. It was wonderful—something like camp meeting. But he could not stay because he had no money and there was no work available for him. He had arrived too late. Much too late!

8

John didn't know what to do. Since he had no return ticket, he couldn't go home. Anyway, he didn't really want to. Staring into the dark, he lay awake in his bunk in the dorm room, making plans, discarding them all. He had come all this way to go to school, but he needed money for that. Very well, the thing to do was to earn some. When he thought of Uncle Malcolm's offer, he rejected it immediately. He had found the school he wanted, and it wasn't Knox College. On the other hand he couldn't be a logger—he knew that already. Yet he had never held any other job.

Uncle Malcolm had been pretty nice, and his father had a sister. Where did she live? In Toronto, not far away at all! Her name was Flora, the same as that of his sister. Maybe she would be as lovable as his Flora. At least he could try.

It took him a while, as Toronto was more than just a little town, but he found her. She seemed just as pleased to see her nephew as Uncle Malcolm had been and offered to let him stay with her while he looked for a job.

Buying a newspaper, he read the help-wanted ads until he found one he thought would interest him. It had been put in by a man who owned a sawmill, and that, of course, was the kind of work John knew something about. He applied, and the man hired him.

To John's disgust, the job had nothing to do with lumber or a saw. What the man wanted him for was hauling fertilizer to his fields, and it wasn't commercial chemicals or even animal dung. It was just plain raw toilet sewage. He lasted one day. The stinking stuff repulsed him to the point where he was physically sick. So he went back to reading the newspaper.

It was almost Christmastime. The stores were putting up their decorations and beginning to advertise seasonal gifts. Noticing several places that were taking on additional help, he was brave enough to go directly to the largest department store in the city—T. Eaton & Company. He filled out an application, and to his surprise, the company employed him.

The store was a place of wonder for him. He had traveled some now, and wasn't entirely a green country boy, but T. Eaton & Company made him feel so totally inferior that he felt he could hardly handle it. Fortunately the store gave him a job as a salesman. He had had so much experience selling books that before the morning was over, he was talking to the customers as confidently as he had knocked on doors, and he felt quite grand representing all the wealth he saw around him. A few days later a floorwalker in the section where he worked came along, patted him on the shoulder, and said, "Mac, I've been observing you. You're a natural salesman. You know, when this Christmas rush is over, we will be getting rid of some of these extras, but I am going to recommend that they keep you on."

John went back to his aunt's house feeling at least two inches taller. He had only one problem. So far he hadn't told his employer that he was a Seventh-day Adventist. He decided that he'd better take advantage of it while he was in favor.

The next day he looked up the man who had spoken to him. Taking his courage in both hands, he started out, "I wanted to thank you for encouraging me. And I wanted to tell you something else, too. I became a Christian not too long ago, and I'm trying to live according to the Bible. That means I keep the seventh day as Sabbath, and I can't work on Saturday. From Friday evening sunset until Saturday evening sunset I must be out of the store." He looked at the man hopefully.

The floorwalker was thoughtful and maybe a little

bewildered. Pausing in what he was doing, he studied McEachern carefully, as though to make sure he was real. Finally he said, "Well, maybe we can fix that up. I'll go and speak to the big boss."

Relief flooded John as he went back to his position. Things would surely work out this time.

He was wrong. The superior would not allow anyone to have rights that the rest of the employees didn't have. "And anyway," the floorwalker added "what's the difference what day you keep, just so it is one day in seven?" He patted John on the shoulder again, then went away saying, "Aw, you'll stay on. We need you, and you need the work. You'll stay by us."

John resumed his job, wrestling with himself and his conscience. Friday afternoon came, and with it the big temptation. The store never looked more beautiful. His pocket never felt more empty. And he dreaded facing his aunt, who would surely laugh at him. Suddenly he straightened up. No use even thinking about it. He had made his decision long ago. Going directly to the office, he collected his pay, saying he wouldn't be back for work in the morning.

Aunt Flora did more than laugh at him. "It's stupid, that's what," she scolded as he ate breakfast the next morning. "You'll never find a better place than that one. Already they were recommending you for promotion, and now they'll never consider taking you back. Besides, how are you going to find another job when people see that you quit two of them already?"

How indeed? It was a miserable Sabbath, all in all. He went to his room to read his Bible for a while, thinking he could find some help there.

"Wonder if I just let it fall open, if maybe God would choose a special verse for me." His thoughts drifted back to the other time he had done that. Funny, he had almost forgotten Anne, and now he could see her face clearly in front of him.

It had been that time Mr. and Mrs. McEwen had befriended him that he had met her. She was their adopted daughter.

When they had helped send him to school and bought him clothes, she had encouraged him and followed his progress through the year. Later, when he had gone logging, she had written to him faithfully.

John had been eager to tell Anne about his experience with the book he had bought from Carr. He had thought she would be excited, for he knew that she was a churchgoer, though a Presbyterian. She had wanted him to know God, too. John couldn't wait to see her, so he had told her of his growing knowledge in letter after letter. At first, she *was* excited, but when he lost his job because of the conviction he had about the Sabbath, she wasted no words in letting him know that it made a great deal of difference to her what doctrines he held. They had had heated arguments.

He remembered that final time. Having delivered his books, he was home from canvassing. The camp meeting had been not too long before. Now there was just the matter of harvest and getting ready for school. Funny—it seemed so long ago, but it was really just a matter of months.

He had come in from the field to get a drink of water, thinking about Anne and how to win her over to seeing things his way. Suddenly he noticed his mother's Bible, open on the table as usual. Picking it up, he closed it between his two hands, and then allowed it to open where it might, not looking for anything special. The book fell open to Job 31, and the first verse caught his eye: "I made a covenant with mine eyes: why then should I think upon a maid?"

It had been so appropriate to his situation that he had felt instantly that God was reproving him. He had made a covenant to keep God's commandments, and here he was thinking how to get around them because of Anne. Before he even went back to the field, he got a pencil and wrote to her over in Tehkummah, telling her that he had to follow God's Word as best he could understand it.

She had never written to him again. Now, in his present situation, he wondered whether he could find something that would speak to his new problem as that other text had. He was perplexed. Obviously he couldn't go back to Lornedale without any money, nor could he return to his uncle without accepting the offer to attend a non-Adventist school. Furthermore, he couldn't resume his previous job without breaking the Sabbath. Now he knelt, closed his eyes, and prayed for the Lord to guide him and tell him what to do.

With his eyes still closed, he opened his Bible and put his finger on a text. Slowly he opened his eyes, hoping desperately for some counsel. "Choosing rather," Hebrews 11:25 declared, "to suffer affliction with the people of God, than to enjoy the pleasures of sin for a season." Hey, this was great! He read the next verse. "Esteeming the reproach of Christ greater riches than the treasures in Egypt"—that was Eaton's store, of course—"for he had respect unto the recompence of the reward."

For a few minutes longer he stayed on his knees, feeling the sureness flood into him. Of course! Other people before him had had trials like his, and they had been satisfied with their "recompence." He'd just have to stick with the Lord and see what came next.

Monday morning he set out, going from factory to factory, following up every help-wanted ad in the paper. Time after time he was turned down. Finally, toward evening, as he was returning to his room to face again his disappointed aunt, he saw a group of men working on the Grand Trunk Railway.

After watching them for a few minutes, he decided that a certain tall fellow was the foreman of the crew. Walking straight over, he asked him if he needed any more men.

The man looked John over. "It's pretty bad weather, and the railroad tracks are being snowed in. We do need help." He gauged John's size and strength and made up his mind. "Can you use a pick and shovel?"

"Well, I've used a saw and an ax. I think I can use a pick and shovel."

All right. Report in the morning, and we'll provide you

with pick and shovel."

Tuesday morning found John in an old sweater and overalls, toiling with a pick and shovel. It was a far cry from being dressed up as a sales clerk. The men were Italian and talked mostly in their native language.

The work was hard, but John was glad for any kind of work, and every morning found him out wrestling with his tools. Still inexperienced in faith, he didn't tell the foreman he wasn't going to work on Saturday. Monday morning he showed up without an explanation, and to his surprise, no one asked him for one. He puzzled over it for several days, feeling his hands take on thick calluses which they had almost lost after he finished with the plowing. After a few days of listening to the talk around him, John got the answer to his question. Some of the men simply laid off on a weekend, mostly because they spent it drinking and gambling. It was so common that the supervisor just accepted it and shrugged it off.

"I can't let him think I'm like those fellows," John told himself. "I'd really better talk to him."

He decided the same thing every day, but it wasn't until Friday evening that he finally marched up to the foreman and began to talk to him about his belief in God and his need to keep God's law. "Sir," he finished, "I did not come to work last Saturday, and I cannot work tomorrow, for I worship on the seventh day as God requires in His Ten Commandments. It says . . ."

A burst of positively blistering swearing interrupted John. "None of that nonsense around here, Mac. You work Saturdays or you go to the office and collect your pay." He turned his back.

John was utterly discouraged. Maybe God didn't want him to go to school. Maybe he should buy a ticket back home to Manitoulin Island. At least he had that much money now. He should go before the bay froze up.

Monday he was on his way to the ticket office at the Toronto train station. Idly he thought about people he knew, and wondered suddenly where his friend Carr was. H. D. Carr right now would probably be knocking at somebody's door, telling whoever answered about *The Coming King* or about those prophecies in Daniel. Yes, the man would be selling books somewhere.

Like a blinding flash of light it came to him finally. Why, John McEachern could sell books, too. No need to ask for Sabbath privileges. A smile spread across his face, and when the ticket agent asked his destination, John bought a passage to Lornedale Academy. Perhaps he could find a place to live there while he canvassed. At least he'd be with people who wouldn't scorn him for his firmness in his beliefs. And if nothing worked out, he could say Goodbye to several acquaintances he had made among the students.

The first one to greet him on campus was Elder Leland. "John! Good to see you, man! How have you been getting along?" He shook John's hand warmly. "We've been worried about you in that big city. The students have been praying for you. How is it going?"

"It's been rough," McEachern replied. "Every single job I got I lost because of the Sabbath. Even the railroad job, although I was almost the only one sober sometimes. But I've decided to sell books. I can do that on my own time. I've had some experience at it, too."

"Of course!" The principal shook his head ruefully. "Why didn't we think of that before? Why, you can stay right here, attend classes, and sell books after school hours and all day on Fridays. Maybe you can work your way through school selling books!"

John felt warmed right down to his toes. No one had ever given him such an enthusiastic welcome. Again he felt the faint ache inside that was always there when he thought about what he never had had from his father, but it vanished in a second, like the early-morning mist. They wanted him here. Here he would stay.

That same day John finally enrolled as a student. Because a

law in Ontario prohibited working on Sundays, school met from Sunday through Thursday, leaving Fridays for the heavy duties and shopping that by law the school body could not do on Sunday. So on Fridays and after weekday school hours John canvassed. He put his heart into it, and suddenly the tide seemed to turn. His books sold well—so well, in fact, that he earned enough to pay for all his expenses and still had time to make up the studies he had missed during first semester. It was too good to be true.

His books were handled through the conference's Tract Society in Toronto, so whenever he picked up new books, he went to the offices there. Generally being in quite a hurry, he seldom noticed who served him. But one day was different.

"Excuse me," the young woman at the desk said. "May I ask you a question?"

John stopped what he was doing and looked down into a pair of clear, bright eyes. "Of course," he replied.

"How do you pronounce your name?"

He pronounced it, wondering what it was all about. She was neatly dressed, her long hair swept up in back. He didn't know what to call the arrangement, but it gave her a touch of simple elegance that he really liked.

"It's just that one time I wrapped a book—*The Coming King,* it was—and I sent it off to that same name with a logging-camp address. I thought the name was very unusual, and now that I see you have it, I thought you could tell me how to say it. I've been wondering all this time."

"Really? You were the person who sent it?" John remembered that eagerly awaited package and the reading that followed. Suddenly he glanced around for a chair to pull up. There wasn't any. The young woman was still looking at him expectantly, so he added, "I wish I could tell you what the book has meant to me. You'd be glad you sent it!"

She smiled. "I'm glad already."

He smiled back, then remembered suddenly that he had an appointment to meet. "I've got to go now," he began, then flushed a little. "I really do. I have a customer waiting. But I'll come back one of these afternoons and tell you all about it."

John went out the door whistling, aware of the pair of eyes that followed him. He'd make his orders smaller now, and then he would have to come back more often. His smile lasted all the way down the street.

9

Summer was just around the corner when John found the president of the Ontario Conference waiting for him outside the classroom. At least that is how the man introduced himself, and McEachern took his word for it.

"John," the man said without any preliminaries, "we want you out in a gospel tent effort this summer, starting as soon as school closes."

"Gospel tent effort?" His eyes showed his surprise. "All I know about tents is the camp meeting I went to last summer. I have no experience with tents."

"Oh, you won't be alone, John. You'll be getting experience while working with an ordained minister as he holds gospel meetings under a tent. All you have to do is aid him in setting it all up. You'll help people get seated, pass out songbooks, sometimes have the prayer, give a Bible study. The minister needs just your good assistance. The conference will provide your board and room as well as a bit more toward other needs." The president smiled and added the clincher. "We'll see that you get back to school next fall, John, and in time, this time."

McEachern grinned. "What can I say?" He spread out his hands.

"Good. We'll be expecting you."

The president was right. John got his experience that summer. Armed with a missionary license from the Ontario Conference, he learned what it was to pitch a tent. He sprinkled sawdust, arranged benches, passed out songbooks—all the things the administrator had told him about. But with the experience he had had meeting people every day in his bookselling, he was soon discussing, persuading, giving Bible studies, sharing parts of the service. Here, he realized, was what he wanted to do with his life! This is what he was studying for! The pleasure and satisfaction inside was so great that sometimes he thought he wouldn't be able to hold it in. So he didn't. He began to write letters to that young woman in the office. Her name, he knew by now, was Ruby Myrtella Hartwell, though she went by Myrtle. And wonder of wonders, she actually corresponded back. All in all, it was a most satisfactory summer.

It came to an end, and fall and winter sped by. John kept so busy with his studies and bookselling, as well as his periodic visits to the office of the Tract Society, that graduation rolled around almost before he realized it. He didn't know whether to be glad or sad about it. Myrtle was moving to the States with her family, and John did not know yet what was to become of him. So far he had a high school diploma and owed nothing. But he had no profession yet.

Once more the Ontario Conference knocked on his door. John recognized the president this time. "You have another tent job for me?" He smiled.

"Sure do. Your own, this time." Seeing the expression on McEachern's face, he hurried to add, "with plenty of assistance, though. You can have someone to help you pass out the songbooks, put up the tent . . ."

"I know, I know," John nodded sagely. "Sprinkle the sawdust, arrange the benches, give Bible studies . . ."

They both laughed.

"An organist, too, if you like."

Suddenly John's eyes took on a thoughtful look, but he didn't say anything.

"You accept, then?"

"I guess so. If I have good help, I suppose I could do it."

"We'll count on you then," the administrator said, holding out his hand. And then as he turned to leave, he added, "By the way, be sure to let us know where you want to set up your tent."

"You want *me* to choose?" John asked in surprise.

"Right. You choose."

The conference president left. John didn't go out to deliver books that day—he had too much to think about. Several ideas hammered away at his mind, and he wanted plenty of time to think them over. There was so much at stake.

Sitting there on the porch of the boys' dormitory, he reviewed many things in his mind. He saw himself again, a boy of fourteen with black teeth and a seething anger in his heart, heading down the road, running away from his own father. A second time—leaving home in the middle of the night, vowing never to return. Dark memories, blows, the strap, sharp words, the ever-burning fires of hell.

Another memory: standing at the door of his cabin, seeing for the first time what age had done to his father and mother. He relived the day he had forbidden his father to strike his mother. The green cornfields, the new house, the comforts he had sought for his parents—one by one the events ran through his mind. Once more his father sent him to hell when he became an "Advent." And below all the memories, he felt the familiar ache.

He was older now, more mature, and realized as he hadn't before his great need to have a relationship with his father. Also he now recognized that the man that was his father had been forged in the stern, unloving rigidity of beliefs he had come to accept as his own. John no longer could find it in his heart to condemn him. As with most men, Deacon McEachern was a product of his time and environment. Now John wondered—and it was truly a question to puzzle over—Could his father change? After all, anyone who saw God as a stern Judge wanting only to pronounce the death sentence, how could that kind of person give or receive love? If his father knew that God *loved* him, that He was a merciful Father, waiting for

His children to come home . . . would that make a difference? He pondered it over and over again.

And even if John were to go home with his tent, would his father listen to him? After all, he believed that all Adventists were hell-bent.

Then there was that other little matter. Myrtle could play the organ. Was there any possibility . . . ? They were so close in their goals, wanted the same things for the future. Was now the time to ask?

As evening settled over the campus, he finally stood up. Time to quit thinking. Time to start planning.

"I want to pitch my tent in front of the church where I used to go to Sunday school," John told the conference administration. "I want to let all my old friends and neighbors know what God has done for me and give them the same message that has changed me."

"Fine," came the answer. "Go right ahead."

"And about getting an organ . . . ?"

"No organ this time. Maybe next."

Well, that settled both questions without any hassle at all. Maybe the time wasn't ripe for him and Myrtle. He went on with his plans.

The previous summer all he had had to do was show up and follow what he was told. Now he had to plan, and that put extra pressure on him. He didn't want *anything* to go wrong. Too much was at stake.

He found he was a little homesick, too. It had been more than two years since he had been home, and he was eager to get back. This time he would not be walking home on a dusty country road or across fields along cow paths. Instead, he would be riding in a wagon. Wagons would haul the large tent, the benches, the boxes of supplies. John wanted everything looking good. Everything neat. Everything well organized. He was going home, and what was it Jesus had said about the prophet in his own country? It would be hard, he knew. But he was hoping and praying, for suddenly, more than anything else,

74

he wanted to open his father's hard heart. Wanted to make room there for the love of God. And for a son's love. He wanted what he had not had his whole life long: to know a father's love.

10

The summer sun was slanting beyond the bluff when John's wagons rolled into the village. The wheels made little puffs of dust rise and settle as they turned on the dusty road, and the fields were beginning to brown a little in the heat. John watched nervously for the turn in the road that would open into the gate of his home cornfield. Pulling out a handkerchief, he mopped the sweat off his forehead. His feet wanted to run ahead, but the butterflies in his stomach pulled him back. He had written that he was coming and mentioned what he was going to do, and he wasn't certain what kind of reception he would get. Once again he mopped his head, then put his handkerchief back and looked around.

Things hadn't changed too much. The church was there with its bell in the steeple. The houses were scattered and sparse. The bluff broke where it always had, and suddenly John wondered idly whether chokecherries still grew on it.

Rounding the turn, passing the gate, the horses plodded down the entrance and stopped obediently. The front door opened. It was his mother. Forgetting his newly acquired dignity, he ran up to the steps to hug her.

"Oh, it's good to see you, John," she told him in a voice that trembled.

"It's so good to be home, Mother. I've missed you!" He held her at arm's length to get a good look. She was more frail than ever, and his heart jerked inside him. "How is Father?"

"Same as ever." Her eyes twinkled up at him. "He won't

admit it, but he is rather proud to have a preacher for a son."

John smiled with relief. "Will he come to hear me?"

"I'm sure of it, son." She put a finger to her lips. "But don't you mention it to him."

"I won't, then," he agreed, glad to dispose of the subject anyway. "I'll settle the things, and then I'll be in."

McEachern had a lot to do before he could start any preaching. The next day he went into the village to secure permission to pitch his tent opposite the church. A little concerned about it—for by now it was well known that he had joined the heretical sect of the Advents—he practiced his speech several times, trying to choose just the right words, but he need not have bothered.

"Sure you can use that space," the owner told him jovially. "Let us know what we can do to help, if there's anything."

So it was up with the tent and down with the sawdust. It took a full day to get that done and the benches placed in order. Also he had the advertising and community visits to make. To his surprise, John found little opposition. He realized he owed some of that to the fact that his father was a deacon and therefore a respected member of the community. Life is so ironic, he thought to himself as he made the rounds. I always hated my father's church position and his religious outlook, and now it's actually helping me.

The other thing that helped him was something he did not realize. The neighbors could not but remember how as a teenager, John had used his logger earnings to provide his parents with a better home. They had seen him toiling out in the fields for no profit of his own, and they respected the ideals that had impelled him to those actions.

Another surprise awaited him at home when he returned from his visitations. "Phemie! What are you doing here?" he exclaimed as he walked in the door and saw the sister sitting by the kitchen table talking to Elizabeth.

"I just had to come home and see what you were up to, John," she teased. "They say you're planning big things, and I didn't want to miss them."

"Why, you . . .!" He broke off with a laugh and hugged her instead.

John had really absorbed a lot that summer he had helped with meetings. He had learned a pattern of programs, a method of dealing with people, a series of sermons. Now he would use them in much the same way for his own meetings. Some things would be different, though. His biggest burden was his own father, and more than anything else he wanted for the Holy Spirit to change that heart. He spent plenty of time out near his bluff in the early mornings, pleading for the Lord's help as he spoke. Also he asked for a lot of patience, as he knew quite well what he had to deal with once he was out of the pulpit and back at home.

The first night he was a little nervous as he left for the tent. Would anyone come? Sure, they had all said they were interested, but maybe they were just being polite. Also, what if his father didn't really mean to attend?

He need not have worried. People began to straggle in well before time, and the benches were pretty well filled before he recognized the little group that slipped in quietly and sat well toward the back. It included not only his father but also both his sisters and his brother-in-law. Bowing his head, he gave thanks.

John began his series telling about God. He presented Him as best he could, showing His great love for a lost world. He showed the Creator carefully forming man in His own image, tenderly blowing the breath of life into him. He told of His pain when sin destroyed that image and of the great love that was willing to suffer separation, ignominy, and death on a cross. The young evangelist put all he had into it, and in the upturned faces he could see the Holy Spirit at work.

In successive meetings he explained about the terrible damage sin had caused, not only in the world but in the character and personality of man himself. He revealed the great desire God had of restoring His image and of insuring the happiness and prosperity of His children. He talked about the law God had given as a safeguard to this end and what that law taught. One time he spent the whole evening on the fourth commandment, explaining its importance in the God-man relationship. At that meeting he gave his very first altar call.

"You have seen God's love for you," he told them all, "and the way He has provided you with a means of salvation. You see now what God asks of you and why. I would like to invite you now to respond to His love. If you would like to show the world that you do love God and that because of this and of your conviction of His love for you you will keep His *whole* law from now on—if you truly desire this—I ask you to come forward."

His eyes swept across his audience, wondering who would be the first to have courage enough to respond. It wasn't easy—he well knew that. He was about to offer up a silent prayer when he saw a movement at the back. Someone was already stepping out into the aisle. After staring unbelievingly at the old man walking toward the front, he left the pulpit. It was his own father! With wet eyes, John stepped off the platform and took his father into his arms with a son's joyous hug.

"I'm sorry, John," the deacon was saying. "I've treated you so wrong. I have believed such wrong things about God. Can you forgive me, son?"

Could he forgive him! Why else was he here?

John never forgot that night. The whole congregation felt the emotional impact of the deacon's astonishing reaction. One by one others joined the two there in the aisle, stirred in a way they themselves could not understand. After a few moments his sister Euphemia walked up to the front too.

When the meetings ended, McEachern stayed on to hold Bible studies with the people who had made their commitment to God on that memorable night. To his great joy, his father and his sister never faltered. At the end of the studies both asked for baptism.

"I do so thank You, Lord," John whispered on the day he

saw them lowered into the water.

So now he had part of his family with him in the Adventist Church. He could have worships with them, they could keep Sabbath together, they could go to camp meeting together. It was like being reborn for John. He had a father and a family now. Oh, maybe he and his father wouldn't see eye to eye any better than they had before, and maybe there would still be harsh words and disagreements. After all, he couldn't expect the old man to change into a different person overnight. But still it was wonderful.

To John's surprise he had underestimated his father.

"We've got a lot of time to make up," his father said one day quite simply when John showed his surprise over a quiet, agreeable answer he hadn't expected. "I reckon we can still do some things together, you and I, son."

"I've wanted it so much, Father," John answered, choking up a little.

"I know, boy. Seems like I just couldn't, before . . ." His voice trailed off.

John didn't know whether he dare reach out his hand and put it on the deacon's shoulder, but he sure wanted to. "It's OK. I know how it was, Father." He didn't touch the old man—not yet. But he knew the time was coming when he would. The time when he would have what he had longed for and then prayed for.

Meanwhile he had other things on his mind. John had another tent meeting series to hold, and the conference asked him to go to a locality that had a larger population. He also learned that they would permit him to use an organ.

He lost no time in writing Myrtle to let her know that he badly needed an organist to aid him in his meetings there. "No one there is an Adventist," he wrote, "so I have to look elsewhere."

She had no doubt about who should be the organist, and she must have told him as much, for by return mail he suggested that she come up to Sault Ste. Marie. He would meet her there, they could be married, and she would join him and Elder Walter Hancock in the tent meetings.

But he hadn't reckoned with a few obstacles, and one of them was Myrtle's parents. "If that young man wants you bad enough," her mother stated firmly, "let him come down here and have the wedding."

John didn't know that Myrtle was the only child of a well-to-do couple. Her father, Sperry D. Hartwell, was the conference auditor at the time, and was used to his daughter going out with some rather sophisticated suitors, young men with a secure income and a definite future. Myrtle's mother had in mind someone with cultivated tastes and refined manners. A newly converted lumberjack was just not their idea of an ideal partner for the girl, and things in the Hartwell home were not exactly peaceful when Myrtle announced that she had lost her heart to the young man in question.

John didn't get his organist that summer. Not only that, now he had to find a way to save up enough money for his trip to her home—supposing they could work things out to get married—money for the tickets for two of them to come back, a release from his work for time to make the trip, and all the other items accompanying the addition of a wife to his schedule.

"It'll take several months," he reported regretfully to her. "I hate to wait so long, but it's probably for the best."

She accepted it philosophically, perhaps a little relieved to have the extra time to prepare things—not to mention for the attitude of her parents to soften. When it came to the announcements they were going to use, she found herself staring at the name: John H. McEachern.

"H'mmm. Wonder what that H stands for," she mused. "Must be Henry." She left it at that, jotting down in her mind a reminder to ask him later. John would remember the rest of his life the shock it gave her when he informed her that the H stood for Hector, not Henry.

In fact, it became a family joke that he told each of the children with a grin, remarking, "It's a good thing she didn't ask until after the wedding. She might have taken that as the last straw, what with her folks objecting and all . . ."

But in the meantime John had to get on with his duties. Those several months of waiting were going to be busy ones for both of them—months in which much would happen to strengthen their commitment to each other.

11

Summer ended, and John went right on into the fall helping Elder Hancock with meetings. The highlight of every day was the moment he went to check the mail and see what it held for him. Seldom was he disappointed. The envelopes he took from the counter were his lifeline, and after reading them, he carried the letters in his pocket wherever he went.

"You don't want to marry a girl from the States," a church member told him one day. "There are nice girls in Canada. In fact," the man lowered his voice confidentially, "I have just the one for you. She's an only child, and her parents are very well off." He paused to watch the effect of his words. "When they die she will inherit all of it, and just think how you could help the work prosper here in Ontario!"

McEachern stared at him unbelievingly, but the man seemed quite serious. "Uh, thank you very much." John tried to keep politeness in his voice and manner, but it was a struggle. "I really have made up my mind already."

The "person" lost his smile. Frowning a little, he offered, "Well, perhaps you'll think it over." Then he suddenly discovered he had another errand to do.

Christmas came and went. Taking down the tent and stacking the benches one cold evening, John felt discouraged and suddenly a little fearful. What do I have to offer her? he mused as he began packing hymn books into a box. Look at my own home! I don't even know what a real home is like! I've never seen the Christian wholeness, the love and tenderness, that is a home. How can I create one myself?

Eventually, though, his spirits began to lift as though the weather affected them. Each day closer to spring made him happier, and finally, he was able to write home. "We will be married on the twelfth of March in Battle Creek. I do wish you could be there . . ."

"It's not much of a honeymoon," John explained to Myrtle as they rode the jerking train. "But it's an institute for people who sell books as I used to, and I was especially invited."

"It's OK, John," she said, squeezing his hand with a knowing smile. "You don't have to apologize. I know it's really important to you, so it is to me, too."

John settled back happily. He looked out the window at the scenery and thought how fortunate he was. From feeling like a loner in the world, he had gone not only to having a real father but a wife now, too! Better than that, she seemed to understand how he felt about things.

The colporteur institute convened at Kalamazoo, Michigan, not far from Berrien Springs. John enjoyed every meeting. Elder J. B. Blosser, general canvassing agent for the Lake Union Conference, noticing that McEachern was from outside the States, asked him to give a demonstration as he had been accustomed to doing it in Canada. Feeling at home among all those people who shared his experience in selling books, John walked right up onto the platform and did the best he could to show one of his approaches.

"You're enjoying yourself, aren't you?" Myrtle commented that night when he came in from the last meeting.

"I sure am! I didn't know there were so many fellows out selling books!"

"They're not all booksellers," Myrtle informed him wisely. "In fact, some of them are here for quite different purposes. There's an Elder Lamson from Emmanuel Missionary College, and he wants to talk to you as soon as possible."

"Whatever for?"

"Ask him."

"Someone with drive like yours should be in college, John," Lamson told him the next day when John finally located him. "You could do so much with an education. There's no limit to what you could do for the Lord."

"I've always wanted to go on with my education," John admitted a little bashfully, "but I don't have the money. Especially now. I have a wife to support."

"There's bound to be some way," the college president persisted. "Talk it over with Myrtle. Maybe you can figure something out."

The meetings went on another full day, but John's attention was divided now. His imagination had been fired up. "I could study anything, Myrtle," he told her excitedly. "I could go straight through college and then on into medicine. I'd really like to be a physician."

"Why not?" she encouraged him.

"Why not?" he echoed. "There are a lot of reasons why not. For one thing, I haven't any money, and education—" He stopped. "Why are you laughing at me?"

"You were putting on your preacher's voice," she teased him. "Getting all wound up to deliver your sermon. Why don't you sell some books, silly!"

It seemed to be the answer he always came back to: Why don't you sell some books? With her encouragement, John went back to Sault Ste. Marie to canvass. In three weeks' time he had sold enough books to pay a year's tuition, and by autumn they were on the campus of Emmanuel Missionary College.

"Say Hello to Dr. McEachern," he chortled that evening as he came in from registration. "I'm all signed up."

"Everything is working out just fine, John," she affirmed. "I'm sure this is where the Lord wants us to be."

John entered his studies with the same eagerness he had always had for books. This time, he was sure, he was going to get to learn all he wanted to, and nothing was going to stop him. He knew how to earn all the money he needed, things were going fine at home, and he had someone to stand by him and help him through his hard times. But he had forgotten about some people who hadn't forgotten about him.

One late afternoon a knock on the door interrupted John's class. The professor, a little annoyed, stepped to the hall.

"I wish to speak with John McEachern," the visitor said.

John was puzzled. Who could be wanting him? And whatever for?

It was the president of the West Michigan Conference, and he evidently did not have the same outlook on education that Elder Lamson had. "We need you out in the Lord's work, John," the man said. "You have no time to be here studying things you don't need. The Lord is coming soon, and we need workers out there. You've had a lot of experience, and that is important. Won't you come and work with us here in Michigan?"

John smoothed his dark hair thoughtfully, all his fine plans beginning to disintegrate. He listened while the administrator talked on and on, and all the time he wondered what in the world he was supposed to do. Finally he shrugged. "You're the president of the conference, and I guess I'm subject to your orders," he decided finally—feeling that God used the chosen leaders to direct and employ, but wondering why the Lord hadn't intervened before he had started out on his career. "I guess I'll come, but let me finish out the school year first, OK?"

The president agreed reluctantly, and John went back to his studies. But now, on the side, he made charts and plans, getting ready to go out in a tent series in the summer.

In the meantime, things turned even more complicated. The Lake Union Conference had met in session in Chicago, and the states of Wisconsin, Illinois, Indiana, and Michigan had each given a report and presented its needs. East Michigan was desperate for a man to head their book distribution efforts. They had only one lone salesperson. The conference leaders and the Lake Union men felt that it was the greatest need presented yet.

Then Elder J. B. Blosser, who had been at the Kalamazoo

Colporteur Institute, stood up. "I know just the man for you," he told the union committee. "You get McEachern for the East Michigan Conference, and I think your troubles will be over." Then he explained why. The union committee didn't waste a lot of time discussing. They simply passed on the recommendation that the West Michigan Conference release McEachern to the East Michigan Conference to become the leader of their publishing program.

Poor John! He wasn't even out of school yet. West Michigan had asked for his services, and he had promised. Now the Lake Union had told it to release him, but the conference just deferred the decision, leaving it up to John. "You go on over to the conference meeting in Flint, and look things over, but you don't have to accept the job there. You're called to the ministry," the leaders stated flatly.

In his confusion, John went to Flint, Michigan. There he came under a lot of pressure to accept the position as their publishing leader. The nominating committee must make its report the next morning, so they would have to have his decision by then. And if that wasn't enough, Ontario contacted him with the plea that his own home country needed him back.

"What shall I do?" he asked the man at whose home he was housed. "They're all official calls. I can't be all three places at once. What does the Lord really want me to do?"

"Well," the deacon he was staying with said, "remember back in Bible times when they didn't know what to do, they cast lots."

John considered that one. It sounded as good as anything else, so he took three slips of paper. On one he wrote "West Michigan," on another "East Michigan," and "Ontario" on the last. He put them all into a hat, shook it, and told his host he would remove one slip at a time, then replace it and draw again until he had gotten the same slip twice.

Closing his eyes, he drew out the first slip. Both men craned their necks as he opened it. West Michigan. Good! That was where he preferred to stay. Folding it, he put it back in.

His friend shook the hat, and again John took one. This time the slip said East Michigan. With a shrug John refolded the paper, and replaced it. The three little papers did their funny little dance, slipping and sliding over one another, gliding through the air and coming back to rest. John shut his eyes and picked, fully resigned to getting Ontario this time. But the paper said East Michigan.

The two men looked at each other. "Well," John said philosophically, "I guess that settles that."

In the morning he went to the committee and made them happy by his acceptance, little aware that he had truly cast his lot. He was never to become Dr. McEachern. Never again to pull the saw in a logging camp. Never to receive his B.A. as a theologian and preacher. Instead he was now called a "field missionary secretary," and he had not the faintest notion what that was supposed to mean, nor did anyone seem to know what he was supposed to do or where he was supposed to set up headquarters. But when he set out from that committee meeting to find Myrtle and tell her the news, his feet were placed firmly on the path of the booksellers, men like his friend Carr who had first told him of the coming King. Who had not only opened up his understanding to a God of love, but who indirectly had given him an earthly father, too, and had uncovered the gift that lay inside him—the gift of salesmanship.

EPILOGUE

John would live a long and fruitful life in the profession chosen for him that day, but he always considered the three highlights in his life as having occurred before that. The first, of course, was when, with his friend Bob, he discovered that God was not the deity of his father. John's God loved him and wanted to save him. The second was the day he gained what he had longed for all his life—a father in the real sense of the word. That evening when his father walked down the aisle of the tent into his arms and God's was the moment of his greatest miracle of joy. The other highlight, his marriage to Myrtle, was one that lasted for forty-one years, and sustained him through the many hard years of constant work and challenge, for the publishing program was small and unrecognized then.

The first thing John did was to go out looking for salespeople. He went to Oshawa and found two men to bring back with him. Then he journeyed to Greenbush, to Bay City, to Holly and Vassar, to one place after another until he reached Detroit. Within a month he returned to the conference office with a list of forty men ready to solicit orders.

The second thing John did was to hold a preparatory institute, where he gave explanations, instructions, practice, and then actual experience in selling books before assigning a territory for his men to work in.

After the institute, John himself set the example. He went to a county where one lone Adventist lived. She, a Mrs. Rice, had appealed to the conference for the church to do something in her area. John walked six miles to get to her home. They talked of her neighbors and their religions. Mrs. Rice had the feeling that the people were prejudiced and bitter toward her.

After staying with Mrs. Rice for the noonday meal, he walked a half mile to her nearest neighbor. Unaware that he had already visited Mrs. Rice, the woman told him, "You may not know it, but my neighbor up the road is a Seventh-day Adventist. She is a wonderful person. Her girls are real ladies. They do not frequent dance halls and movie theaters, and they are always modest in their deportment and dress."

By noon the next day he ate with Mrs. Rice again. John went back to her home not only because he could have a porkless meal there but because he wanted her to know how much her godly life had impressed the neighborhood. Her way of living had helped him take orders for books. He showed her a whole page and a half of names already in his prospectus as proof.

Farther north it was not so easy, for he learned he was now in a community of spiritualists. At one home where he arranged to spend the night the family gave him the guest room to sleep in. The moon was shining, and the night was beautiful. He chose, however, to stay inside and study awhile before retiring because someone always asked him to preach on weekends. After a bit of organizing and planning for the morrow, he turned the wick in the kerosene lamp low, and he lay down to sleep.

During the night he heard noises in his room and wondered what was happening. As he turned, thinking of lighting a lamp to find out, a hand clutched his throat. There was no arm, no wrist, but a tight fingerhold. A voice said, "I'll teach you to meddle with spiritualism," and clutched tighter, choking him. Desperate, John managed to breath the word *Jesus.* The muttering ceased and the clutching hand lifted.

The next morning at breakfast with his host, he mentioned the noises he had heard. The man had feared there were such things. Also he had heard rappings. His mother, he said, had died a short time before. She had gone to spiritualistic seances previous to her death.

John told of his release by uttering the word *Jesus* and, after a short Bible study on the subject, had prayer with him before leaving. He had occasion to use those same Bible texts with others that day as he canvassed.

One aspect about his work irked John. "Book agent" was bad enough, for a book agent could sell novels or any kind of trash. A canvasser could solicit for political votes, people's opinions, and such things. John wished those he was helping and supervising could have a more honorable title, for they were truly ministering the word of God. It humiliated him to have others introduce him before he preached in a church as "John McEachern, our state canvassing agent." He was not serving a state, he was not an agent—certainly no state agent—and "canvasser" was a distasteful term to him.

After directing the publishing program in Ohio, Pennsylvania, and other places, he advanced to a position in a union conference. There he used his persuasive eloquence to get himself and others in such positions called "Union Field Missionary Secretary."

Being a union conference official, he went as a delegate to the General Conference Spring Council at Loma Linda, California, in 1915. There, assigned to one of the committees, he had opportunity to press his point about a change of name. He wrote up a resolution and talked with others about his views. Then he approached W. A. Spicer and A. G. Daniells. They said, "Mac, we never thought of that. It's a good idea. Put it on the agenda of the committee for plans and bring it before the session."

John prefaced his written resolution with a preamble, stating that in earlier times people selling Bibles and religious works had been known as colporteurs. He noted that Mrs. E. G. White used that word in such connection and that she had used *canvasser* by way of explanation.

After the committee cleared his resolution, it went before

the council and was unanimously passed there. Henceforth, those who went from door to door selling Seventh-day Adventist literature and Bibles were to be known as *colporteur evangelists*. The fact that the council met on the campus of the recently founded College of Medical Evangelists may have had its influence in the decision.

One of John's favorite texts was Proverbs 18:16: "A man's gift maketh room for him, and bringeth him before great men." Maybe its author had in mind sending things to influential persons to win, for his own gain, that person's favor. But to John that verse meant that a man's inborn *talent*, cultivated and utilized, would find him his proper place in the world.

That sense seemed to explain to him why, after he chose to earn his education by selling, he never had to ask for a job again. That inspector at Eaton's had told him, "You're a natural salesman." Canvassing—colporteuring—gave him a marvelous chance to cultivate that talent, and he certainly was a colporteur evangelist, for he did a lot of preaching on the side. You might even say that he sold the idea of the colporteur program to a lot of people. He was as successful in recruiting as he was in selling books. Before he could get enough colporteur evangelists busy in one conference, he would receive requests from others.

For example, while he was yet in East Michigan Ohio wanted him. For six weeks he helped a man there get organized and equipped for leadership. Central Union asked for him. Kansas especially needed help. Before the school year closed he went to Union College in Lincoln, Nebraska and also to the two academies in Kansas to line up a group of young men to spend the summer selling books to pay for their next school year. John, of course, not only prepared them for it but went right along with them to see that they got it done.

One of his student colporteur evangelists once remarked that Elder McEachern saw to it that each group was up early and out to work so as to put in a full day. He personally would be at their door to remind them that "lying in bed won't pay for a scholarship." Those words became almost a slogan with them.

A long dry spell hit Kansas that summer, the worst in years. The discouraged farmers hesitated to order anything, especially books. At the end of one such disheartening week John went alone down to the banks of the almost dry Solomon River and knelt. He prayed for all the young men he was supervising, he prayed for himself as their leader, he prayed for the people who had ordered books, but his big burden was the thing that seemed to be the biggest hindrance to summer success for them all. The land was dry. The crops needed water. So John prayed for rain. For that phase of God's work to prosper in Kansas that summer the soil needed moisture and needed it at once. He told God about it and asked Him to send rain.

And John believed it would rain. Joining the others where they were housed for the weekend, he said to them, "It is going to rain."

"No." None had seen any sign of a cloud. All echoed, "No."

But it did rain. Before morning the whole state of Kansas had had a rain that promised abundant harvest.

John McEachern's gift of recruiting and training colporteur evangelists took him to various parts of the world. About 1918 he went, with Seventh-day Adventist General Conference credentials, to the South American Division with headquarters in Buenos Aires, Argentina, as publishing and home missionary secretary.

World War I was not yet over at that time, and in his new capacity John had to travel much by ship. Submarines were the great menace by sea, and every ocean-going vessel had to prepare for such emergencies. Once, while he was a passenger on a United States liner, the crew told the voyagers that if anything suspicious should threaten, they would give a siren warning. "We all went to bed," John wrote, "wondering what would happen to us in the night." In the afternoon of the next day, while passengers played deck games, the boat's whistle gave a terrific shriek. Everyone ran for the lifeboats. To their relief they discovered that it was just a drill, to let them know what to do in case the real thing happened.

Elder O. Montgomery, in his report as president of the South American Division in the 1919 *Seventh-day Adventist Yearbook,* stated: "The arrival of several new workers to connect with the different fields has been a source of strength and encouragement. Among these new recruits were: Elder J. H. McEachern, who comes as secretary of the publishing and home missionary departments, and Brother E. Everest, as manager of the publishing house. With the larger plans for and better organization of these departments, and this strong general leadership, we look for such an advance move in these departments of our work as has never been seen before in South America."

John would repeat his success in South America in many other places. For ten years he served overseas, and his home address became such places as Manila, Baguio, and Singapore, for he had to cover a territory that embraced Japan, Korea, Formosa, the Philippines, Vietnam, Cambodia, the Federated Malaya States, Borneo, and the Netherlands East Indies. He traversed the vast area an average of twice a year, attending meetings and conferences, traveling by ship most of the time. But always he was still following the trail he started out on with Mr. Carr on that dog sled so long before.

During his term of service in the Far East his customary long work hours overtook him. Three doctors at a Singapore hospital diagnosed his condition as "exhaustion of the central nervous system."

A bleeding ulcer sent him into a comatose condition. Hallucinating, he seemed to be attending his own funeral, and reached into his casket and took out money to pay the mortician.

His wife, Myrtle, had heard one of the doctors say the case was lost. "I'll be back later," he said, "to sign the death certificate." Immediately she hurried to phone the director of the Seventh-day Adventist school in Singapore. He happened to be away, but the students, learning from her that Elder McEachern was near death, quickly gathered and prayed for his healing.

When the doctor returned he found his patient still alive. "Call it whatever you want to, but there's something miraculous here," he told Mrs. McEachern.

That ulcer did cause John to return to the United States of America for a while to rest up and drink carrot juice at Loma Linda Hospital.

Then, after some months of recuperation in their newly established home in California, he accepted an invitation to assist at several New England camp meetings. The effort was perhaps too soon, because the ulcer insisted on hemorrhaging again, and he had to allow himself to be nursed back to health at New England Sanitarium and Hospital in Massachusetts.

After a month of forced stay under medical care, he became impatient and wanted to go home to his family in California. The doctors finally consented and wired his wife, Myrtle, that they were allowing him to take a train headed west. He would be in bed on a Pullman, for he should be quiet all the way. Since he would have to transfer in Chicago, an ambulance would meet the train there and would carefully take John from one train bed to a second train bed.

The ambulance met the train in Chicago all right, just as the doctors had planned. But they found no McEachern. He had dressed, had left his bed and the train, and had made his own way to California. It seems he felt an extra strength once he was homeward bound, for the story goes that a political convention had convened in Chicago, and John did not resist the urge to find out what it was all about before continuing his journey.

The Singapore experience was a precious thing to John—something like his "born-again" feeling in the logging camp. He treasured it as he did the gold Elgin watch Myrtle's parents had given him just before the wedding, signifying their acceptance of the suitor they had opposed. Many wonderful things had come into his life after he gave himself completely into the hands of the God who loves. Now, near the close of his life, he thought about them all with real gratitude. Then he sat down and wrote

THE POTTER AND THE CLAY

How good it is to be resigned
To weal or woe by God designed.
He is the Potter; we the clay;
Let Him mould us as He may.

When clouds arise to dim our joy,
These are His means to cleanse alloy—
A rainbow bright shines o'er our head,
Though dark the pathway looks ahead.

Sometimes we're tempted to be sad,
But Christians always should be glad.
God's promise true, O claim the fact!
All things for good will sure react.

When wealth takes wings and friends forsake,
Position gone, and health at stake,
Look up and know that God is King,
You're still His child; rejoice and sing.

Some day beyond this vale of tears,
When life is measured not by years,
We'll shine as vessels, tried as gold,
And praise the Potter's every mould.

John sleeps in Jesus now. Deacon McEachern sleeps too, having died finally at peace with a loving God.